THE
QUIET
OF
MIND

Strategies & Methods Proven To Help You Find Your Inner Peace, Accomplish Your Goals, And Live Your Dreams

JAMES BROOK

Copyright © 2024 James Brook

All rights reserved. No part of this publication may be reproduced, distributed, or transmitted in any form or by any means, including photocopying, recording, or other electronic or mechanical methods, without the prior written permission of the publisher, except in the case of brief quotations embodied in critical reviews and certain other noncommercial uses permitted by copyright law.

Contents

Introduction v

Chapter 1. The Beauty Of The Mind 1
- What Is A Neuron And How Does It Work? 3
- What Happens With A Healthy Brain 6

Chapter 2. The Challenges Of The Mind 9
- Worries On Repeat.........................11
- Losing Your Breath........................12
- The Insecurity Of A Busy Brain..............13
- Dreamt Up Disdain 15
- Derealization.............................16
- Weariness, Too 17
- Panic Attacks 18
- Generalized Anxiety Disorder (GAD).........23
- Lack Of Focus 24

Chapter 3. How To Clear The Mind....................28
- Mindfulness 30
- Breathwork..............................33

- Meditation 39
- Apps That Help Quiet The Mind 47
- Self-Talk 50
- Get Good Sleep 54
- Nourish Your Mind, Body, And Soul 56
- Exercising 61
- Journaling 65
- To-Do Lists & Calendars. 78
- Pursuing Hobbies 82
- Seeking Help 86

Chapter 4. What Are Your Goals? 93
- How Do You Figure Out Your Goals? 96
- Keep Progress Of Your Goals 99
- The Benefits Of Meeting Your Goals 102

Chapter 5. Mindfulness 108
- How To Achieve Mindfulness 110

Introduction

Sometimes, it feels like your mind just cannot slow down.

Sometimes, it feels like someone flipped a switch in your brain and that it is moving a mile a minute and there is simply no way to stop it. It doesn't matter what the thoughts are - from the grocery list you're writing to the tasks you have at work to the phone calls you have to make or what you'll make for dinner or your plans for next week, month, or year - but they are an avalanche that tumbles through your mind for every single hour of the day.

It doesn't matter how smart or talented you are, there are many days when your brain doesn't seem to listen to you and creates a chorus of nonstop noise that you cannot silence.

And what happens when your brain is acting like this? What are some of the side effects that can not only affect your home life but also your career as well? Unfortunately, there are plenty. Your output at home and at work can suffer and you can become far less of a family person as well as a reliable employee. And, because of that, you could lose friends, family members, and your job.

But there is even more that a restless brain can cause. You can feel like you are utterly exhausted at all times, even if you have gotten a full eight hours of sleep. You'll feel like you are dragging yourself around. You'll feel like every task is monotonous and slow. You'll feel like you have no attention and you have a short temper. In general, you just feel like someone who is spread too thin. Grumpy, irritable, incompetent and just in a bad overall mood at all times.

Who wants to live like that? No one, of course. But for those of us who have a nonstop mind, this is a common occurrence.

Your brain is your biggest asset. It can provide you with great opportunities, wonderful memories, and the sort of life that you have always wanted. But at the same time, your brain can also be your worst enemy and it can be the biggest road block to feeling carefree, balanced, and truly happy and comfortable in your own skin.

That's the double-edged sword that is the human mind: there is nothing more important than it, but also nothing more detrimental than what it can do.

Think about all of the good that comes from your brain: without it, you wouldn't be capable of accomplishing anything. All of the good grades you got in school, all of the advancements in your career, all of the wonderful relationships that you have built over the years - they are all the products of your brain, which creates the sort of person you are. Your personality is heavily influenced by your mind, and that is a key element to the life you have and the success you have found.

Yes, your mind is the reason you're able to build relationships, have a job, achieve your goals, and live your life happily and healthy. You should be very thankful for it and for all that it has given you. And you should be protective of it and caring for it. You should view it as the very vital asset that it is.

At the same time, there are few problems and issues as big as the ones that can be set by your own brain. In that way, it can be your own worst enemy.

Some people don't have this problem. Some people go through life only experiencing the very good that comes from their minds. They don't have to battle with their own brains at every turn and every day. But then there are the rest of us, who simply do not have it that way. And for us, we have to learn how to adapt and outsmart our very own minds.

Because, if left unchecked, the brain can do some truly brutal and painful and frustrating things to us and our lives. Not only is the brain the one place that all your anxieties, fears, paranoias, and doubts come from, but it's also a place that can easily get cluttered with thoughts, plans, and too much information. It's like a filing cabinet that can never get full enough. If you let it, your brain will just continually get fuller and fuller and fuller. But instead of a filing cabinet that is jam-packed with papers and reports, your mind is overloaded with thoughts, fears, paranoia, questions, doubts, and so much more.

And even though it can be loaded with a seemingly endless amount, there will come a time when your brain feels like it is downright fit to burst and cannot hold one more piece of information.

Think of all the things that you place in your mind each and every day, even when you're not thinking about it. Everything you know, everything you hear, everything you think about and ponder, all rests inside your brain. That is a lot of stuff so you can understand how it might get weighed down, bogged down by all of that information.

Again, if you are reading this book then you are not like other people. Certain individuals have the ability to somehow filter through all of the stuff they interact with during the day and aren't compelled to lodge it all in their minds. But that's not us. We bog ourselves down with every moment, every memory, every piece of information that our brain tricks us into thinking is vital and important for the future.

And when it does get bogged down and fit to burst with so much stuff, your entire life can suffer. You will have a harder time holding down a job, a much more difficult time making and maintaining relationships, both friendships and romances. Plus, you will not feel comfortable in your own skin. With a busy, cluttered mind, you will feel out of sorts, rushed, worried, unsure of the next step to take.

THE QUIET OF MIND

You cannot find peace without a peaceful mind. And you cannot have a peaceful mind if it is packed to the brim, cluttered, and messy.

What is a cluttered brain? In short, it's a mind that feels like it's a mess. It's a mind that retains every thought, conversation, and moment from every day. But a cluttered mind doesn't just hold onto these images and memories, it repeats them, it keeps them in the forefront, it doesn't have the ability to truly let them go.

And the cluttered mind can obsess better than typical minds. It can replay moments, it can convince you that you did something wrong or you didn't perform correctly. It can make you second-guess yourself, think lowly of the person you are, and generally live a life filled with paranoia.

A cluttered mind has a skill and it's this: tiring you and making life harder.

In some ways, having a cluttered mind is something to be proud of. Why is that, you may ask? How could having a cluttered mind be possibly considered a good thing? Well, because only those who are creative and intelligent have the capacity in their brains to think so much. Of course, it's usually a detriment and should be avoided, but a cluttered mind means that you have a highly powerful brain that can process things quickly and move with ease from one subject to the next, usually to a fault.

JAMES BROOK

When you think about a cluttered mind, you can understand why so many people are fearful of it. You can understand why people would do whatever it takes to turn things around, get better control of their brains, and silence the loud noises that seem to never stop. Decluttering your brain is something that doesn't just feel important but downright essential when it is constantly proving to be the biggest enemy you have in your life.

Good thing that there are ways to declutter your brain.

That must be a huge relief for you and you may be excited to get to work and learn how to finally control and silence the rabid beast that is your brain. But you should know a few things. Firstly, it takes work. It doesn't happen overnight. Decluttering your mind is about finding your inner peace and accomplishing the very attainable goals that you have. But all of that requires proven methods that you have to learn, and practice.

It's not enough to just say, "I want to declutter my mind." Instead, you have to put in the work - and there is a decent amount of it.

But we will show you all you need to know and we will teach you the practices that so many others have used over the years. These methods look different to everyone, they vary from person to person. For some, it's about making lists and making sure every item on it is checked off, one after another. For others, it's about meditation and practicing gentle self-care exercises like deep breathing, guided meditation, and exercise. For even more, it's about being held accountable by smartphone apps or friends.

THE QUIET OF MIND

The act of decluttering the brain definitely does look different from person to person. But to find the way that works best for you, you need to explore and be educated about them all. Then and only then will you be able to really get a handle on your brain and become the master of your own mind.

Before we get to the hard work that is waiting for you, it is important that we give you an uncomfortable image to think of.

You come home from a long day of work. You are dead on your feet, so tired and so ready to eat some dinner, take a hot shower, set your alarms, and crawl into bed in front of your favorite TV show. You have earned a good night's rest and you're going to get it, right?

Wrong.

Because of the way your mind works, your leisurely evening is actually filled with flashes of moments throughout the day and a million reasons why you acted inappropriately and embarrassed yourself. You are also thinking about what work will bring you tomorrow and what new, fresh horrors await you when you wake in the morning.

Instead of relaxing in front of your favorite television show, you are instead pacing around your home, unable to sleep and nervously fretting about the days and weeks ahead. Before you know it, it's 3 in the morning and you haven't had a wink of sleep yet.

JAMES BROOK

In the morning you wake, even more tired than the night before, dragging your feet to work and it's the same the day after that. You don't feel like yourself. You feel grumpy, nervous, jumpy, and unhappy. Your brain is wearing you out and, sadly, it just won't stop.

You would think that your mind would be as worn out as you are and would not be able to function at such a high speed. Yet, even though you are utterly fatigued, your brain continues to hurl more and more horror at you. And it doesn't stop.

This is what a cluttered mind looks like. This is what you are sadly very used to. And this is what you want to change.

And this is what you *will* change, based upon the lessons you will learn in the chapters ahead.

In the pages of our book, we are going to teach you all that you need to know about decluttering your mind, freeing up your thinking space, finding peace in your body, and setting aside mental and physical space to remain calm, remain steady and meditate in order to remain in a good mind space all of the time.

When you put this book down, you will not be cured of a cluttered mind. Unfortunately, this is a part of you that will remain forever. You cannot simply cut this part out of your body and the way that you work.

However, you will have the tools needed to traverse through your mind's unrelenting speed and habits. You will know what to do when your brain flares up and starts to act out. You will find the methods that work best for you and then you will use them. Like a tool bag full of items that can get the job done, you will now know what is needed when the bad times come.

You will not be cured. But your brain will no longer be able to push you around like it used to. You will be able to push back, and truly fight in ways that you never have before.

And, over time, you will see that it takes work but calming your mind and finding your peace even in the worst of times is possible.

We will go over strategies and methods that millions of people have used to find a mind that is free of excess noise and distraction. We will go over these methods, teach you how to use them, and also talk about the results that can come from it. By the time that this book is over, you will have a whole playbook of things that you can try when your mind decides that it is going to give you a tough day.

Tough days will still exist, make no mistake about that. But you are going to be able to deal with it in ways you couldn't before.

Let's dig into it all. Let's talk about how the mind works, the hidden chemistry that goes on behind the scenes of your brain, the way that a cluttered mind manifests itself during your life and your job and beyond. Let's talk about all of the good, the bad, and the ugly that comes with your cluttered mind.

There are methods to calm the mind. There are ways to ensure that it doesn't have the last say in the way that you feel. These ways have worked for millions of people for thousands of years. They have been waiting for you, and now it's time to learn all about them, master them, and then master your mind too.

There is little joy to be found with a cluttered mind. But this is not something that you have to be sentenced to for the entirety of your life. You can combat it, you can fight back, you can become the bigger and stronger person you have always suspected you are.

Your peace awaits. Your happiness awaits. Your life, as it should be, awaits. It is time for you to learn how to fight for it and finally silence all of the noise that mutes everything else and declutter your brain.

CHAPTER 1

The Beauty Of The Mind

When you really think about it, your mind has been the companion with you through thick and thin and during all things since the beginning of your life. And not only has it been there with you during every event, both big and small, but it has also shaped the way that you see the world, see other people, and see yourself.

There is quite literally nothing else in the entire world that has the sort of impact that your brain does.

Think of every single happy memory that you hold near and dear to your heart. Remember all of the good times with family, friends, and co-workers. Remember the laughs that you had, the joyous exciting turns of events that you didn't see coming, the quiet moments that you will forever remember fondly and turn to when life is stressing you out or pressing down hard on you.

There is no doubt that those moments were legitimate, real, and truly special. But they only hold significant value to you and your heart because of your brain. It was your mind that saw everything, defined it, conceptualized it, and held onto it. It was your brain that let you feel that joy and allowed you to create those memories.

Yes, your brain can sometimes feel like your worst enemy - especially when it is crowded and filled with so much clutter like an unkept desk. But your brain is also the thing that allows you to feel joy, make memories, and live a life that you are happy about.

The brain does a lot, doesn't it?

In its most basic sense, your brain is like a little supercomputer that rests inside your head. However, unlike the modern supercomputers that are used by high-tech, billion dollar companies, your brain is completely free, and only yours.

But the way that it works and manages just so many tasks and performances is startling and worth learning about. It is really quite stunning to find out just how the brain works and it's one of the most beautiful things about it.

The composition of your brain and the way that it is able to learn so much, tell you so much, and control so much really starts with a neuron. Without neurons, your brain wouldn't be able to function as it does, for better or worse. These neurons are smaller than anything visible to the human eye but they do so much and they perform such necessary tasks that they are thought of as the most important part of your brain.

What Is A Neuron And How Does It Work?

The brain is filled with a seemingly endless amount of highways and byways and pathways filled with these neurons, all of which are communicating with one another and helping you function, learn new things, and turn something that was once new and frightening into old habits.

There are so many neurons running through your brain that trying to count them is just about useless. Your brain, which is roughly just a bit bigger than your clenched fists put together, holds billions upon billions of these neurons, all of which are functioning at all times and talking to one another, passing each other messages, and keeping your body moving.

Did you know that there are in fact more neurons in your brain than there are stars visible in the night sky with the unaided eye. Although the official number of neurons in your brain isn't 100% agreed upon by scientists, it is thought that there are about 86 billion. And what exactly is a neuron? Essentially, a neuron is a type of brain cell that communicates with other neurons by giving them nerve impulses, which are similar to electrical signals. They are connected to one another, communicate with one another, and work together as a cohesive unit in order to make the most basic functions of your body go without a hitch.

Without neurons, your brain wouldn't be able to do the most basic, elementary tasks. Things that you take for granted wouldn't happen. For instance, when you write, brain cells tell others to "use your fingers," and these other cells pass this instruction on to your fingers. An entire system of connected neurons speak to one another in just a tiny split second in order to make your fingers move, your feet walk, your mouth open, and your body perform the necessary, simple things that you do a thousand times in just 4 hours.

Your brain contains a vast range of these connections and resembles an extremely dense spider web due to the connections that each neuron may make with up to 10,000 other neurons. Studies have examined the human brain and have seen this dense, endless array of neurons light up like a city skyline at night when they are functioning. To look at a brain scan is to see the most intense, complicated, and important web of inter-connected neurons relying on each other and talking to each other.

Neurons are a key component to you learning new things, whether that be playing the guitar, working at a new job, or even remembering a new friend's name. Your brain undergoes significant changes when you are learning things, including the creation of fresh connections between your neurons. Scientists refer to this phenomenon as neuroplasticity.

Have you ever heard the term "practice makes perfect"? Well, that's incredibly true when it comes to neurons learning and working in your brain. The connections they make get greater -

and stronger - the more that you practice any given task or habit. The communications from neuron to neuron are transferred quicker and more efficiently as your connections get stronger. Like a muscle that you strengthen when you are working out at the gym, they become more reliable and stronger when you use them more in your daily life. The growth strength of the neurons in your brain is how you improve at whatever you study, including sketching, dancing, baseball, and more. The more you do it, the better you become and there is a scientific reason behind that.

Think of the last time that you took a hike through the forest and the point when you hit a rough patch that hadn't been maintained and cleared of growing nature. Without a clear route, it can be challenging to navigate the vast wilderness since you have to struggle through the untamed grass, shrubs, and brush. Your legs get cut up, your limbs are bitten by bugs, and you might feel defeated and lost and like there is no way forward to where you are trying to head.

However, getting through that overgrown path will get simpler the more you utilize the same trail. But if you decide to stop utilizing the path, everything returns to the way it was and the trail you created gradually fades away.

Similar processes may take place in the brain when you cease using a skill. Eventually, the connections between your neurons might be pruned or disassembled. In other words, they become overgrown just like that nature path that we talked about. This is why, if you haven't read a book all summer, it could seem so challenging to pick up reading again and you'll have trouble remembering what was going on in the book and what you learned.

Although that isn't good news, all hope is not lost because certain neural networks have the capacity to become so powerful that the connections or traces never fully vanish. So you should never think that all memories and skills are lost and gone forever because there is a chance that they can come back.

What Happens With A Healthy Brain

There are times when your brain feels like the best friend that you have.

You know what it's like to have a good day. You spring awake in the morning, go bounding into the day, and feel like you are having just a wonderful afternoon where you are accomplishing everything you want, are efficient at work, and feel like you have a good attitude.

You don't feel bogged down by worries, anxieties, or fears about your life or your job or anything related to either. Nothing seems to slow you down. And if and when roadblocks appear during the day, you move right past them.

When a brain is functioning like that, the results are endless and all very beneficial and positive. If you have a brain that works in that way, then you probably had very few challenges when you were in school, and among others in your social circle, and as you grew into adulthood and started to create a career and a life for yourself.

A mind that is working like that is one that isn't cluttered. And a decluttered mind is capable of some amazing things. Reading, arts, crafts, and so much more are possible if you have a brain that isn't constantly filled with the overbearing and nonstop noise of worry, anxiety, and more.

What does someone with a decluttered mind look like? You have seen them before, perhaps multiple times. In fact, there may have been a time when *you* were someone with a decluttered mind, only to have it seemingly lose the ability to stay that way.

Inner peace and a seemingly endless supply of patience come with a decluttered mind. But there is even more that comes with it. If you have a brain that is free from the pressing and nonstop weight of anxiety and stress, then you will be more attentive in just about every part of your life. You'll be better at your work, you'll be a more reliable and closer friend and family member, and you'll also be able to accomplish your goals with relative ease. Those who have a decluttered mind are also those who are often outgoing and willing and able to have fun hobbies, enjoy major life events often, have more money, and just generally enjoy their day-to-day lives more.

Think of how a challenging, cluttered mind can get in the way of just about anything you want to achieve in life. You cannot ever truly overcome your brain because, in the most basic and important ways, you *are* your brain. It is the main key to your consciousness and crafts how you see the world and how you view everything, including yourself. There is no escape from your brain simply as there is no escape from your body. You *are* your brain and there is no getting away from it.

Therefore, if you are trying to achieve even the simplest goals, it will prove nearly impossible if you lack the ability to quiet your mind and gain control of it. But if you are able to do those things - and, make no mistake, you are - then you will be able to be the person that you were always meant to be.

When someone tells you that they are peaceful and have found tranquility, what they are really telling you is that they have figured out how to calm their minds and be in control of it. Inner peace and calm is all about having a quiet mind and that is all about putting in the work necessary to have it.

Having a decluttered and calm mind is a key to a happy, successful, fruitful life. But having the opposite leads to a life that is chaotic, painful, and hard to manage. If you have lofty goals in life, such as the sort of career that you want and the personal life ambitions that mean a lot to you, then you need to be able to keep your mind in check. However, that is obviously easier said than done. But don't fret because it *is* possible. You just have to learn how to do it.

CHAPTER 2

The Challenges Of The Mind

With a decluttered and calm mind, you can find great success in work, in life, and in everything you dedicate yourself to. It can be a key element to you feeling peaceful, happy, driven, and ready to wake up and conquer each and every day with enthusiasm and zest.

And what happens when you have a challenging, troubled, cluttered mind?

As you can imagine, the exact opposite will occur. Life will be full of many speed bumps, roadblocks, and detours. Even the simplest and most straightforward task could be very hard on you and can seem nearly impossible.

A cluttered mind will feel like being in the middle of a massive speaker that is blasting the loudest music imaginable. You can't focus, you can't hear anything else, you cannot pull yourself out of it. The sound of your brain is downright overwhelming and impossible to ignore.

One of the biggest problems with having a loud or cluttered brain is that you might not even recognize that you are suffering from one. That is because the brain has a very strong talent at making itself seem normal. You can't always tell that you are being challenged by your brain and, therefore, you don't know what you have to address.

The brain, even when it's at its worst, has the ability to convince you that everything is okay. And if it's not okay, the brain can try to make you believe that things are normal. Yes, you have a lot of anxiety. Yes, it feels like your mind never turns off. Yes, it feels impossible to ignore the pressing and nonstop weight that your brain creates. But that's normal. That's just the way you are. There is no changing that. At least, that's what your brain seemingly wants you to think.

If you have a brain that works like this, you definitely know it. And if you don't, then you aren't going to be entirely sure just how hard it can be. Many people are aware that having a cluttered mind causes you to worry excessively, but until you have experienced it yourself, it is difficult to express how that feels. Ironically, being able to describe your cluttered mind is yet another thing that feels nearly impossible because of it.

THE QUIET OF MIND

Let's discuss what a cluttered mind can look like to the average person. The truth of the matter is that you might actually have one but aren't too sure of it because you don't suffer from each of the symptoms that we describe. But if you can relate to feeling any of these things, there is a strong chance that you have the sort of mind that needs to be calmed, maintained, and taken care of.

Worries On Repeat

It may seem as though your worst worries are playing on repeat in your head due to the constant tension, anxiety, and other mental chatter that comes with having an overloaded mind. One worry could eventually go away, but then you might experience another.

It might get to the point that you are suffering from the same fears every single day. For example, maybe you have a big work-related assignment that is due in a few weeks. For the days before it, you will be certain that you are going to screw up, not deliver, and fail to do a decent job. It will eat away at you, constantly popping into your thoughts, seemingly impossible to ignore.

Then the day will come and it'll be time for you to step up and deliver your assignment. So, you do and it goes well, it goes off without a hitch and you *should* be happy. But, instead, your brain continues to linger on this subject even though it's done. Now you are worried about how well you did, about people possibly not telling you the truth when they said you performed well, and other issues of self-doubt associated with your now-completed assignment.

As you can see, the issue is that the majority of anxieties that your mind creates are irrational. But, for the person suffering from them, they often don't feel irrational. In fact, they feel incredibly real and inescapable. You need to be able to tell them apart, what is real and what is not. What fears are rational and which aren't. Learning to identify when your cluttered mind, rather than reality, is speaking will help you stop these kinds of anxieties, worries, and pressures. By doing so, you can learn to resist your ideas or to cease focusing on them.

Losing Your Breath

There are multiple physical symptoms of having a cluttered, anxious, unstoppable mind. And, again, some of them become so common for the person suffering that they don't even notice when they are experiencing them. But being able to note when your body is reacting to your busy brain is a great way to know when you need to stop, slow down, and use some of the tools we are going to give you to contain your brain.

The rising and falling of your chest, sometimes moving so rapidly as if you just ran around the block even though you have just been sitting still and not exerting physical energy. This is breathlessness and it's common for those with a wild and seemingly untamable brain.

In fact, breathlessness is one of the most often reported physical signs of having a cluttered mind. You can't breathe because your head is too occupied, for whatever reason. Worries and nonstop thoughts about work, home, or the days or weeks ahead can't be turned off and they are weighing down on you and hitting you again and again. The shortness of breath you feel is actually a result of fight or flight, a physical response that was bred into all of us. The fight or flight response in your body was evolved to assist you in being on guard and either fighting or fleeing from actual, life-threatening situations.

Your breathing becomes shallower and faster as a result of the fear reaction so that more oxygen can reach your muscles. Having a crowded brain can cause shortness of breath, which is innocuous yet doesn't feel that way. In the moment, it might feel like you're about to have a panic attack or trouble breathing because of the way that your mind is going so, so fast.

You could experience this symptom as a feeling of choking, suffocation, or difficulty breathing. This sensation may be both unsettling and alarming. In fact, some people who have anxiety or a busy brain have reported themselves to the doctor or emergency room because they feel that there is something wrong with them. Of course, there isn't anything physically wrong. They just have a mind that won't listen to you, or reality.

The Insecurity Of A Busy Brain

Many people say that having a busy mind makes them feel as though they are losing control of their lives. This can lead to them feeling shaky, out of control, and nervous all the time. Even those who have a settled and successful career and home life might still feel like they are barely hanging onto the control of everything they hold near and dear.

JAMES BROOK

A stressed out, loud, and cluttered brain makes you believe that you are not secure and that an inevitable catastrophe is coming right around the corner. Have you ever heard the phrase "waiting for the other shoe to drop"? This is the mindset that people with cluttered minds feel all of the time. They are certain, even with no evidence, that something bad is about to happen and the ability to shut off that voice in their heads and that side of their brains is non-existent. This pressing feel of dread and doom is unstoppable and will work its way into every corner of your life, from work, home, and beyond.

As a consequence of this, many people who suffer from this sort of mindset describe their condition as feeling like they are always on edge. As you can imagine, this leaves the person feeling testy, irritable, unhappy, and unsure of themselves in just about every single way.

At times, your brain might make an effort to persuade you that you are in danger even though you intellectually know that you are not. Those who have agoraphobia, for instance, are afraid of crowds and wide-open settings. Many times they have a brain that is constantly telling them that something bad is lurking right around the corner and that people around them, even those close to them emotionally, pose some sort of vague but undeniable risk.

People who suffer from this can't feel secure outside of their houses because of their problem. There is no reason to feel this way, at least not a genuine one. Still, the mind has a powerful ability to tell them to stay away from crowds or strangers for their own safety.

You could get an imminent sensation that something dreadful could soon transpire even if you don't have agoraphobia. It could seem like you're always looking over your shoulder or trying to get ready for a catastrophe.

Dreamt Up Disdain

When a mind like yours isn't taken care of properly and isn't tended to it can make you feel as though the individuals you're with dislike you, or are angry with you even when they are not. This sort of paranoia is prevalent among people with cluttered brains who don't go through the proper work to take care of them.

An unchecked brain like this has the unquestionable power to persuade you that everything in your life is dangerous. Particularly with social anxiety, people experience a strong worry of embarrassing themselves in front of or offending others.

Have you ever left a social setting regretting a statement you made or action you took? On the other hand, you may have picked up the phone to call the other person to apologize if you committed a social faux pas. It's as simple as that, something that happens to nearly everyone at one point in their lives.

However, if you have a cluttered mind, you could experience this after each and every social encounter, no matter how small or unimportant. You can begin to believe that everyone is against you and that you are the target of social anxiety. Even though this is obviously untrue, it nevertheless seems quite genuine. Or, you could always believe that you didn't perform well and that you somehow embarrassed yourself. How did you embarrass yourself? That will never be entirely clear and you'll truly never have any real evidence of you doing so. But it doesn't matter because the brain in your head will be constantly telling you that you did *something* wrong, even if you don't know what it is.

This can, of course, lead to a very poor image of yourself. People who have very busy and unstoppable brains often hold themselves in a very low regard. They think they aren't capable of great things, whether it's at home or at work. Most importantly, they think that they aren't *worthy* of such good things. And imagine what happens to someone who feels this way about themselves. They aren't going to try, they aren't going to push themselves, and they are going to actively reject good things happening to them because they truly don't believe they are worth it.

Derealization

Derealization, or the feeling that you're not really "there," is an often mentioned symptom for people with this sort of brain and mindset. What does this look like and has it ever happened to you?

Derealization could resemble an out-of-body experience or the sensation of seeing through a fogged glass in your life. Some people who have experienced this claim that they feel as though an impostor has seized possession of their body and that the "genuine" version of them is powerless to stop the imposter from running their lives.

Derealization occurs more frequently than you may imagine, and their main causes are extreme worry and stress. It's something of a coping mechanism created by the body for people who are feeling an immense and insurmountable amount of stressors. Although this sensation might be alarming, counseling can give you strategies to help you regain your sense of reality.

You want to be front-and-center during your life and you want to feel completely in control and as if you're actually living your life to the fullest. But derealization is a guaranteed way to make sure that you don't feel that and it can detract from your life, because it makes you feel as if you aren't really a part of it.

Weariness, Too

No one likes to feel fatigued and out of sorts. Think of the times when you haven't had a good night's sleep and just how much of a negative impact it had on your life. You aren't good at your job, you're not very present when it comes to interactions and moments with your friends and family. You feel tired, you feel out of gas, you feel like you don't have the emotional bandwidth to do anything, let alone form and maintain a strong relationship with people, even those close to you.

This fatigue, also referred to as weariness, is a common sign of someone with a brain that needs to be taken care of and cleansed of excess. It's possible that your brain keeps you up when you're trying to sleep and contributes to your fatigue. That is because you are continually replaying moments from the day or worrying and thinking about what will come soon.

Yet even if you are getting enough sleep, a non-stop brain can make you feel tired. That is because the constant work of the brain takes a lot of effort. You might not always notice it but your brain uses a lot of energy during the day, even though it is doing things that it mastered years ago. This is why good and solid rest is so important: it gives your brain time to relax, sleep, and recharge for the next day.

Imagine a life when you never feel that sort of relaxation or rest. Imagine going into each and every day feeling completely drained and out of energy because your brain has been going nonstop, even when it had no reason to.

Having your brain move a mile a minute all day is tiring. When dealing with the persistent anxiety and stress about your routine and life, every day events will feel draining to you. Although worry frequently keeps individuals awake at night, other people may oversleep, in an effort to suppress their anxiety.

Whether it results in you not sleeping enough or sleeping too much, a cluttered mind is going to wreak absolute havoc in your relationship with relaxation and rest. And that is arguably a bad thing that will lead to diminished results at school, at work, or at home. You need to have a normal, healthy sleep pattern and a busy brain that won't shut off is a way to make sure that doesn't happen.

Panic Attacks

Some people who suffer from a cluttered mind also suffer from something else that is quite pressing and terrifying in the moment: a panic attack. Anyone who has experienced a panic attack knows just how terrible it is. It really does feel like you are losing complete control and that your life's in danger. Those who have cluttered and busy minds are more likely to suffer from panic attacks because their brains are easily triggered and filled with anxiety day-in and day-out.

Hopefully, you have never experienced a panic attack. But if you have, you know the telltale signs of one and how it feels. Essentially, a panic attack is a sudden and intense episode of fear or intense anxiety that pops up seemingly without any apparent reason.

It is a common symptom of an anxiety disorder, such as panic disorder, but it can also occur in other mental health conditions like post-traumatic stress disorder (PTSD). Panic attacks can be very distressing and overwhelming for the person experiencing them. There are many people who call the emergency services or rush themselves to the hospital because they believe that they are in physical risk of death because of the symptoms that they are feeling with a panic attack.

Usually, a panic attack reaches its peak within only a few short minutes. However, it can sadly last for a few minutes to an hour, though some symptoms may persist for a longer duration. During a panic attack, individuals may experience a combination of the following physical and emotional symptoms:

Rapid heart rate
Shortness of breath or hyperventilation

Sweating
Trembling or shaking
Chest pain or discomfort
Feeling dizzy or lightheaded
Nausea or abdominal distress
Feelings of choking or suffocation
Fear of losing control or going crazy
Fear of dying
Numbness or tingling sensations
Hot or cold flashes

Panic attacks can be triggered by specific situations, such as crowded spaces or public speaking, or they can occur unexpectedly without any obvious external trigger. The fear of having another panic attack can lead to anticipatory anxiety, which may contribute to the development of panic disorder.

For many people who have loud and busy brains, panic attacks can become sadly quite common. That is because these are the minds that are predisposed for this sort of attack. The feeling of thinking too much or being inundated with nonstop thoughts and worries is something that happens to most people who have brains that are wired like this.

There are many ways for you to combat panic attacks and an overall goal to declutter your mind through the hard work that we talk about in this book is one of them. But it is also important to remember to seek professional help if you or someone you know experiences panic attacks frequently, as they can have a significant impact on daily life and overall well-being. And what sort of impact can these attacks have?

During a panic attack, the body goes into what is called "fight or flight" mode. During that, the body releases stress hormones such as adrenaline and this might lead to certain physical symptoms like an increased heart rate, plus rapid breathing, chest pain, and dizziness. These physiological responses can be distressing and may even mimic the very real and troubling symptoms of a heart attack, leading to unnecessary trips to the emergency room.

Panic attacks are extremely frightening experiences. The fear of losing control, going crazy, or dying can be overwhelming and lead to severe emotional distress. The aftermath of a panic attack may also leave the person feeling anxious and on edge, worried about the possibility of another attack occurring.

Frequent panic attacks can interfere with a person's ability to carry out regular activities, such as going to work, socializing, or even leaving the house. Individuals may avoid situations or places that they associate with past panic attacks, leading to social isolation and reduced quality of life.

Experiencing panic attacks frequently can increase the risk of developing an anxiety disorder, such as panic disorder or generalized anxiety disorder. These conditions can further exacerbate anxiety symptoms and lead to a cycle of fear and avoidance.

Prolonged stress and anxiety can contribute to various physical health issues over time, including cardiovascular problems, gastrointestinal disorders, weakened immune system, and sleep disturbances.

The emotional toll of panic attacks can strain relationships with family, friends, and colleagues. Loved ones may struggle to understand the person's experience and may feel helpless in providing support.

Frequent panic attacks can erode an individual's self-esteem and self-confidence. The fear of having an attack in public or social situations may lead to a negative self-perception and avoidance of new experiences.

Some individuals may turn to alcohol or drugs as a way to cope with the distress caused by panic attacks, leading to substance abuse issues.

While panic attacks themselves are not physically harmful, the cumulative impact of experiencing them frequently can significantly affect a person's well-being. Seeking professional help is crucial to address panic attacks and any underlying anxiety disorders to improve overall health and quality of life. Treatment options may include therapy (e.g., cognitive-behavioral therapy) and, in some cases, medication to manage symptoms and address underlying anxiety disorders. Always consult a healthcare professional for an accurate diagnosis and appropriate treatment.

Generalized Anxiety Disorder (GAD)

As mentioned before, generalized Anxiety Disorder (GAD) is a mental health condition characterized by excessive and uncontrollable worry or anxiety about various aspects of life. It often goes hand-in-hand with people who have panic attacks and cluttered brains.

People who have GAD usually experience regular, chronic and persistent anxiety that interferes with their daily activities and well-being. The worries in GAD are typically broad and not limited to specific situations or triggers, unlike other anxiety disorders that may be more focused.

Individuals with GAD find it challenging to control their worrying. They worry about everyday things such as work, health, family, finances, and other aspects of life, even when there is no apparent reason for concern.

The worry or anxiety in GAD persists for at least six months, and it is present most days during this period.

Along with emotional distress, people with GAD often experience various physical symptoms, including restlessness, muscle tension, fatigue, irritability, difficulty sleeping, and concentration difficulties. The worries in GAD can be out of proportion to the actual situation or be unlikely to happen, but the person finds it challenging to shake off the anxiety.

The excessive worry and anxiety can significantly interfere with a person's ability to function in their daily life, affecting their work, relationships, and overall quality of life. And GAD often coexists with other anxiety disorders, mood disorders, or other mental health conditions, further complicating the clinical picture.

The exact cause of GAD is not fully understood, but it is likely a combination of genetic, environmental, and biological factors that contribute to its development. Traumatic events, family history of anxiety, and imbalances in brain chemicals may play a role. Of course, those things are often at the core of people who are suffering from cluttered minds too. Therefore, if you have a busy brain, you might also have GAD as well. And when they work in tandem, they can really wreak havoc on your life.

Effective treatments for GAD include psychotherapy, medication, and other relaxation techniques. If you or someone you know is struggling with excessive worry and anxiety, it is essential to seek help from a mental health professional for proper diagnosis and appropriate treatment. With the right support, many people with GAD can find relief and learn to manage their anxiety effectively.

Lack Of Focus

One of the identified symptoms of a brain like yours is an undeniable difficulty focusing. It doesn't matter if you are trying to do some chores at home, trying to finish something for work, or even trying to drive down the road to pick up your child, you will have a very hard time keeping yourself focused on the task

THE QUIET OF MIND

at hand and it'll feel like you're easily distracted and pulled away from it again and again.

Some people who experience this have compared it to trying to concentrate on a conversation or event in front of you while you are wearing noise-canceling headphones. With the headphones on and operating, loud music is all you can hear. Sure, you can make out what is going on around you and you can figure out what's happening but it takes a lot more effort and you are going to miss some key points because of the overwhelming presence of the sound in your headphones.

Your anxieties and fears consume all of your thoughts, whether you're at work or out with friends. How can you possibly focus when so much is pressing down on you, at all times?

If left unchecked, it'll only get worse. And as it becomes worse over time, your difficulty concentrating might start to affect your life in many ways. For instance, you can face disciplinary action at work or begin to drift away from your loved ones. You don't want to act this way and you are doing everything in your power to prevent it but it's nearly impossible to stop because it feels literally impossible to remain focused, even on the things that matter so much to you.

Frequently, worrying thoughts, fears, anxieties, and pressing paranoias will send you on a downhill trajectory like someone skiing on a steep mountain of snow. The initial worry that pops into your hurried head might then soon easily turn into more and the ideas associated with it get progressively more terrifying and pressing. It's called a snowball effect, where something starts small and hardly noticeable but gets bigger and bigger and more and more scary.

Those are just some of the ways that a cluttered mind can make itself known in your life. It can manifest in many other ways, unfortunately. We only touched upon a few physical aspects of having a busy brain but, sadly, there are even more. You might get headaches, you might feel sick to your stomach or you might be completely out of energy.

Whatever the symptoms and the ways that it shows, living in this manner might give the impression that you have no command over your thinking at all. Even though your brain is obviously a part of your body - and a vital one at that - you could feel like your brain is completely cut off from its own animal entirely, and not well within your control at all. Your brain won't feel like part of you, but rather an enemy entity that exists outside of your body, and outside of your control.

Naturally, this isn't entirely accurate. Everyone has some degree of mental control, but it might sometimes feel like you don't. The trick is that you need to figure out the right tools and the right steps to take when your brain is feeling most out of control.

And that is what we are going to learn about in the pages ahead. It doesn't matter how severe the symptoms associated with your cluttered mind are. It doesn't matter how frequently you feel them, either. The truth is that you have the ability, the power, and the purpose to fight back and overcome what your brain is trying to do. It *can* be done. But much like someone who hasn't been to the gym before, your amount of experience doing this is limited. You need to put in the energy and learn the skills needed. Before you know it, you'll once again feel like the master of your mind.

As you can see, the consequences for not keeping your brain in check are intense, overwhelming, and sometimes very detrimental to your life and even your health. No matter your lot in life, no matter your age, and no matter your experience handling mental health problems, you can take control again and get yourself back on track when your brain is not being very friendly to you.

Your mind might try to tell you, often, that you aren't in control and that things are falling apart around you. But the opposite is true: you have *all*, of the control. You just need to remind yourself of that.

CHAPTER 3

How To Clear The Mind

Your mind is filled with things, many of them unnecessary and detrimental to your life.

Even though your mind is capable of some great things and has the ability to make you a huge success in terms of your career and your personal endeavors, it also has the ability to throw multiple monkey wrenches into your life and to make everything so much harder than it has to be.

If you want to find your inner peace, accomplish your goals, and live your dreams, then you need to acquire the tools necessary to clear and quiet your mind.

The bad news is that you have to put a lot of effort and energy into making sure that your mind is healthy and well-maintained. But the good news is that it *is* possible, even if you have no experience with any of this sort of work.

Clearing your mind isn't always easy. But, like all habits, practice makes perfect. That means you have every reason to get started as soon as you can, no matter your age. You should begin to pursue the things that are going to make your life easier and quiet your brain, even when it's at its loudest.

There may be times when it feels like doing this is impossible. As we have mentioned, the overbearing and nonstop cacophony of noise that comes from your brain makes it feel impossible to focus on anything else, even something as easy and natural as sleeping. But the truth is that it's not impossible. In fact, it's very possible.

Think of it this way: you're like someone who has never run a mile before. Even jogging just fifty yards leaves you feeling exhausted and like you're on the verge of collapsing or getting sick. The concept of actually running an entire mile feels impossible when you have never done it before.

But any able-bodied person can actually run a mile, they just need to teach their bodies how to do it. It starts by a little bit of jogging, then you begin to build stamina, move faster, move more, and continue to push yourself more and more. It might take time - weeks, months, even years - but you will someday be running an entire mile. You might actually enjoy doing it. The days of you feeling totally exhausted and drained by just a bit of running are long behind you.

The same is true when you're trying to master your mind and declutter your brain. When you first start, it might feel as intimidating as climbing a mountain as tall as Mount Everest. But with practice and true commitment, it can be done.

Good news: you have plenty of tools to put in your tool bag. Plenty of ways to calm your rowdy brain. Not all of them might work for you but some of them will perfectly fit the bill. So, let's look at some of the proven methods that people use when they are trying to get in control of their brains.

Mindfulness

One of the best ways to declutter your mind and make sure that it feels in control and completely calm is to practice mindfulness. But mindfulness isn't as straightforward as you might think and you might not have any experience with it. It typically involves creating a feeling of awareness in the present moment without any form of judgment about yourself or how well you are doing. All of this can assist you in becoming more present, reducing stress, and enhancing your overall well-being. As you can imagine, it is key to making sure that your mind doesn't feel so overloaded with unnecessary thoughts and emotions.

To achieve mindfulness and a calm mind, you need to allocate a certain time for you to practice it each day. It doesn't have to be a lot and can be just a few minutes when you are starting your day. You can also do this during your lunch break when you are at work, or before you climb into bed.

Whenever you choose to do it, find a quiet, calm, and comfortable place where you are able to sit or lie down without any sort of distractions. Even the smallest distractions can add up and make it much harder for you to really focus like you need to when you are attempting to find mindfulness.

When you are starting the process, you'll find that it's a lot like meditating or breathwork, which will also help keep you calm and settle your busy mind. Start by paying attention to your breath as you inhale and exhale. Notice the sensation of your breath entering and leaving your body. Take it all in, including the sounds of your breathing, the physical feeling, the speed, and more.

Expand your general awareness so that it includes other sensations in your body too, like the feeling of your body in the bed or your feet on the ground or the feeling of your hands which are likely sitting on your lap.

Now use these senses to remain even more present in the here and now and not let your thoughts go to what else you have to do in the day or really anything beyond the present. Notice the sights, sounds, smells, tastes, and textures around you.

Avoid judging your thoughts or experiences as good or bad. Simply observe them as they come and go. This process isn't about stopping what you're feeling or thinking. In fact, mindfulness is about just letting it all come to you and observing it all. You are being mindful of what you're feeling, what you're thinking, and the physical sensations around you.

And if you don't feel like you're gaining any results after you have practiced mindfulness, don't stress out about it too much. Just like any other skill worth learning, mindfulness will improve over time with more practice.

It's quite common for your mind to wander away during this sort of practice. And whenever you notice that this is happening, just gently lead your focus right back to the present without judging yourself or being too hard on yourself.

If you end up finding it hard to achieve mindfulness without help, you should consider using guided meditation apps or recordings that can assist you in leading you through the process.

You can also incorporate mindfulness into daily tasks like eating, walking, or even washing dishes. Even the most monotonous tasks can actually be a way for you to find mindfulness in your day-to-day life. When you are soaping up the dishes, pay close attention to the sensations, smells, and feelings associated with these activities. Don't judge them, for they are neither good nor bad. Just feel them and acknowledge them.

Many people who aim for mindfulness expect too much, too fast. And that is a surefire way to be disappointed with the results when they don't look exactly like you'd imagine or move as quickly as you'd like. Therefore, you need to be kind to yourself as you embark on your mindfulness journey. Let go of expectations and embrace the process of learning and growing. The last thing you want to do is put too much pressure on yourself. If you do this, it'll only add more clutter to your brain and will only make matters worse.

Always remember that mindfulness is not about achieving a certain, strict, specific state of mind. Instead, it's about being present and accepting things as they are in each moment. Over time, with consistent practice, you may notice the benefits of a clear mind, increased awareness, reduced stress, and a greater sense of well-being.

Breathwork

Have you ever heard someone say "Just calm down. Just breath"? There is a reason for that. That is because breath work is a very important practice that will bring you much inner peace and a better handle on your mind, even in the most intense and stressful situations. It doesn't matter how much your mind is throwing at you, controlling and focusing on your breath can go a long way to silencing it at the most important moments.

Breathing can help you feel more at peace, more calm, and it can give you much more clarity. True, everyone breathes countless times every single day but there is a difference between simply breathing and practicing breath work. Let's discuss it and see how it'll look in your life.

Many people call this type of breathing "intentional breathing" because it's all about the intention behind it. And what is the intention behind this method of breathing? Basically, it is to turn your focus away from whatever is troubling you and instead putting it all on the speed and depth of your breathing. Intentional breathing techniques, such as diaphragmatic breathing, yoga breathing, and various other breathing exercises, have been shown to have a range of positive effects on health and wellbeing as well as on quality of life.

What Are The Benefits Of Breathwork?

If your brain makes it hard for you to remain calm, remain focused, and remain happy, then trying out some breathwork might be perfect for you. That is because it is a physical act that works outward in. It revolves around the act of breathing, of course, but it will soon have a real significant impact on your happiness, wellbeing, and the amount of noise in your brain.

What are some of the noticeable and healthy benefits that come with investing time and energy into learning breathwork?

Less Stress

Reductions in stress, worry, and anxiety are among the main advantages of this type of breathwork. By assisting people in ending their stress cycles, breathwork can help people prevent stressful events from triggering their fight-or-flight response, which we spoke about before. That is a learned, evolutionary response to danger. However, for those with a cluttered mind, fight-or-flight might pop up far too often, especially at times when it isn't necessary.

Being a world-renowned mindfulness technique, breathwork aids those experiencing anxiety in centering themselves in the moment while reassuring their bodies that they are safe.

More Energy
Beyond helping your brain be decluttered and remain calm, regular breathwork also has the potential to provide you with more energy. Did you know that your energy levels and immune system are both strongly influenced by your breathing patterns? This shows that it is more important than we may have ever believed. Our bodies may take in more oxygen by engaging in breathwork exercises, and oxygen fuels in our cells that keep us happy and full of energy.

The better you breathe, the healthier you will be, in multiple ways.

Lower Blood Pressure
It has also been demonstrated that breathwork significantly lowers blood pressure, which can be elevated when your brain is acting out and filled with unnecessary and challenging thoughts and worries.

Additionally, it can aid in enhancing blood flow all through the body and even in the management of the condition known as hypertension, which is a killer to millions of people every year. Sadly, people who are often stressed out because of the hardships of their minds are often suffering from hypertension too. This shows that frequently practicing breathing techniques is a fantastic natural way to aid in heart disease prevention.

Manages Pain

An increasingly used technique for treating pain, especially recurring pain, is deep breathing. This, is due to the fact, that numerous breathing methods aid in bringing about a sense of calm in tense or challenging circumstances, and using these techniques as directed also serves as a form of diversion. This enables breathwork to add to a happier mood, which is advantageous for people who are enduring physical discomfort.

There is a reason that people who have suffered an injury immediately start breathing slowly and loudly. That is because the body knows that breathwork can help you feel less pain, even if it's severe.

Improves Your Self-Esteem

We mentioned before that people with busy brains often have a low image of themselves because they often don't feel worthy of any sort of respect or love and they do not push themselves to try more and work harder because they don't believe they can achieve anything substantial.

But many individuals who practice breathwork elevate their state of mind and increase their self-image and the care they feel for themselves. It has also been proven to improve your confidence too.

Breathing exercises can assist people who struggle with unfavorable thoughts and feelings, particularly ones that are self-directed, stay grounded in the here and now. Additionally, the calming feelings contribute to the development of peace. Breathing may enhance our feelings of joy, thankfulness, and happiness while also improving how we perceive ourselves.

Improves Sleep

To aid in bettering their sleep is one of the other main reasons why many people are turning to breathwork. Breathing exercises will help you manage your level of energy so you are able to sleep well every night. Numerous exercises can also assist you in settling for the evening or in falling asleep quickly at night when you have trouble doing so.

One of the top suggested natural sleep aids is breathing exercises, which may also be beneficial for people who are experiencing insomnia.

Manages Your Depression

Additionally, breathwork has shown promise in managing depression when combined with other therapies. It is tremendously beneficial in efforts to enhance mental health and cultivate gratitude because of its capacity to modify one's mood and aid in keeping people in the present moment. Higher breathwork techniques frequently emphasize healing, which is also quite helpful for individuals who are having trouble.

How To Start Breath Work

It's clear that working on your breathing can greatly enhance your ability to control your brain. Because of that, it might be the key to living a much better life. If you master breath control, you could possibly be able to control your mind too.

With such promise, you could be ready to get started with your breathwork. But if you have never done this before in your life, you might have no idea of where to start. Of course, you breathe all day, every day, but how do you set time aside and really focus on the useful art of breathwork?

The good news is that getting started isn't hard at all and you can soon inject this calming technique into your day-to-day life as soon as possible. To make it easier on you to try, we have some time-tested and easy-to-follow tricks that will help you start your journey with breathwork and therefore, your journey to better decluttering your mind. As you will see, it's not nearly as hard as it may seem.

Start Slow
The most crucial thing is to begin gradually, modestly, and then work your way upward. It's important to train your neurological system. If you haven't gone a mile, you cannot complete a full marathon. Novice breathers ought to avoid lengthy meditations and set a clock for one minute. As you become accustomed to breath work, lengthen the time.

Focus On Your Belly
Your upper chest and back won't move noticeably when you're breathing deeply. Your low belly expanding and contracting is an

indication that your diaphragm is working. Practice pressing and pulling with a hand on your tummy.

Remember, You're Doing It Right
Regardless of the approach, merely the act of focusing on our breath helps to close the gap between the parasympathetic and sympathetic systems of the brain. Breath work eliminates more carbon dioxide from the body and fills the cerebral cortex with oxygen, and you cannot mess it up.

Do Whatever Works For You
There are several strategies that can assist you in achieving the ultimate aim of your breath work practice, which is to engage and relax the brain. Find the one that you enjoy and can use frequently and stick to it. Don't feel any sort of shame or pressure to do something that doesn't feel right for you.

When you find what works, commit to it and attempt to put it into your daily routine.

Meditation

There are many people who practice both breathwork as well as meditation too. Once you have studied both, you will see that they go hand in hand and carry many similarities. One benefits the other and while they seem to be cut from the same cloth, there are differences.

When it comes to breathing, it's a rather simple exercise that you have experience with. After all, you breathe all day. But meditation is a bit different. However, it is still about quieting your mind, as well as opening it up too, depending on the method that you follow.

Meditation has been used by millions of people for years now and they have found a strong sense of inner-peace because of it. In fact, entire cultures have been built around its importance. But even though it is wildly popular throughout the globe, you might not be very familiar with it.

Let's discuss meditation, how it works, and what it brings to your life and your mastering of your emotions.

Meditation is an activity which entails employing a mix of mental and physical approaches to focus or cleanse your thoughts and calm and center your mind.

You may practice meditation to unwind, lower anxiety and tension, and more, based on the kind you select. That is why many people employ it. However, we are going to have you use meditation as a means to soothe your brain and make sure that it is manageable and quiet.

There are many various types of meditation, which have been practiced for thousands of years. We are going to focus on just a couple of them that are best used for gaining control of your thoughts and silencing your very noisy, seemingly unstoppable brain.

It has only been in the last couple of decades that contemporary science has begun to thoroughly examine this practice. Technology has enabled many of the major advancements in science's knowledge of meditation. That means that even though we know a lot about meditation now, we will learn even more about it in the years ahead.

The thing that is so important to remember about meditation is that there are many ways to do it. There are in fact countless studies and schools of meditation that people follow. Which one is right for you depends on the one that gives you the results that you seek.

If you practice these two types of mediation and find that you really like them, you should branch out and try others. But since our book is about decluttering your messy mind, let's start with the two schools of meditation that are most appropriate for doing that.

Concentration Meditation

Concentration meditation entails concentrating on one thing, as you may have expected. This could involve paying attention to your breathing, reciting a chant or a single phrase, gazing at a candle flame, hearing a gong strike repeatedly, or numbering beads on a mala. The goal of this type of meditation is to focus your mind on just one thing and attempt to shut out the noise of the world and all of the emotions flowing through your mind.

If that sounds like a large task and something that you might not be able to do the very first time. That's because it is! It's a lot to ask of someone, even someone who has a lot of history with meditation. Because it can be difficult to control the mind, a beginner may just meditate for a short period of time before increasing the time.

Start small and start slow and then begin to build your way up if you are enjoying meditation. As always, show yourself grace and don't be too hard on yourself if it doesn't click the first time.

Something important to keep in mind, at all times, is that your mind is going to make it hard for you to focus and concentrate. That is expected in really any form of meditation. But there are tricks and techniques that you will follow when this occurs. In this type of meditation, whenever you detect your mind wandering - and it will - you simply bring it back to the chosen object of attention. You just let any and all fleeting thoughts go instead of chasing them down and pursuing them. Your ability to focus is enhanced during this time. They will come up and you will push them away.

This can be a tiring form of meditation because your mind is going to be trying very hard to pull you in every other different direction. It is going to remind you of work, of your grocery list, of things you need to do at home, or promises you made to friends and family, and so much more. If you are someone who has a very busy mind that seems to never stop, you might think the idea of batting away these various thoughts is impossible. It's not impossible but it certainly takes a lot of work.

Some people find that they try this type of meditation and they are so overwhelmed the first time that they never attempt it again. The onslaught of emotions, feelings and thoughts that crowd their minds is just too much and they don't want to even try. That is why you should definitely try this a few times before you make any serious judgment call. It might not feel great the first time but that doesn't mean it won't feel better the more you attempt it.

Another form of meditation that many people use is one that actually acknowledges and in fact invites all of the thoughts that come to you. For some people, this might be overwhelming and could feel like too much. For others, it's the exact type of practice that can create inner-peace and put many of the thoughts to rest by minimizing them.

Mindfulness Meditation

The practice of mindfulness meditation helps the participant to pay attention to assailing ideas and emotions as they traverse the mind. The goal is to just be conscious of every thought as it occurs without engaging with them or judging them.

If you practice mindfulness meditation, you are able to observe the patterns in which your thoughts and emotions typically move. You might gradually become more conscious of the propensity for people to categorize experiences as either positive or negative, enjoyable or painful. A sense of inner balance emerges with practice.

Guided Meditation

The practice of guided meditation is influenced by the voice of the instructor or guide. A lot of us feel it is simpler to concentrate and unwind when our brains aren't completely left to their own ways since our minds have a propensity to roam where it wills. In group settings, this type of meditation is frequently taught by a facilitator, or by recordings that are made available through apps, podcasts, DVDs, CDs, etc.

For novices, guided meditation provides a great place to start. A meditation practice requires the mind to be focused on right now and self-awareness, which might be challenging for someone whose mind is accustomed to wandering.

Being present in the moment without actively doing a single thing or trying to solve an issue might seem unachievable in our rushed and high-stakes world that seems to be always focused on objectives. A guide will give guidance while you are meditating. The guide's voice and directions may be followed, which serves as a diversion from other distracting ideas.

Although not every guided meditation is the same, the majority of sessions and recordings have a few traits. Firstly, your guide will aid in your relaxation by encouraging you to breathe more deeply and release tension from particular muscle regions.

The guide may urge you to imagine your bones and feet developing roots into the earth during what is called a grounding exercise. Actively paying attention to your breath or pulse will be one of the ways you are urged to be in the present. The guide can ask you to picture a healing light enveloping your body and banishing any disease or bad energy.

You could even be asked to picture sending healing light to people who have wronged you in the past during the more intensive guided meditations. In order to bring you back, the guide will ask you to wriggle your feet and fingers and gradually concentrate on your breathing.

There are many additional methods of meditation. For instance, a daily meditation routine followed by some monks, places a strong emphasis on the development of compassion. In order to do this, unfavorable situations must be imagined and changed through the use of compassion. Additionally, there are active meditation practices including tai chi and walking meditation techniques too.

So, what is the best way to meditate? Is there an actual process you should try to follow if this is your first time attempting? Well, everyone is different. But for those who have never tried to meditate, here is a procedure to follow when you are dipping your toes in.

Firstly, you want to find a quiet place that you can spend some time in. While there are people who are able to meditate in the middle of a loud room or a crowded train during rush hour, most people can't do that, especially not at the very beginning of their meditative journey. So you will want to find a place that is relatively quiet and isn't going to be full of distractions.

This means that you will need to put your phone away and also turn off loud noises such as the television or music. Don't worry, you'll be able to come back to them soon. Just the act of excluding those things from your life for a few moments might go a long way to help you feel more centered, calm, and free of anger. But this is when the real meditative session begins.

Here is another thing to keep in mind before you start meditating: you need to be comfortable. It is vital that you sit down - or lay down - in a position that feels good to you. You need to pick a spot and a position that feels good for you and your body. Why? Because you know how hard it is to focus when you just aren't feeling comfortable.

Some people believe that you have to be sitting in a certain position when you are meditating but the truth is that you just need to find what works for you. Don't consider other peoples' choices or hold yourself to some sort of standard. Just do whatever feels good for you.

In your first meditative session, you should aim to just do it for a few minutes. Don't be disappointed if you don't last more than five minutes. Remember that you are just getting started and you need to give yourself grace and allow yourself room to grow. If things go well, you'll be soon meditating for a lot longer.

After you are done, take some time to think about what worked and what didn't. What felt good to you and what felt wrong? What do you want to try again? Was it a rewarding experience? If it wasn't, that's not the end of the world. Don't give up just yet. You should definitely try a few more times before you make any solid judgment about your future with meditation.

For millions of people, meditation is a very important part of their lives and a great tool to use to keep their emotions in check, remain calm, stay focused, and bring clarity and good judgment into their lives.

Apps That Help Quiet The Mind

You might think that you can't just silence or quiet your mind on your own. You have been using the same brain for decades, after all. You can't just suddenly change the way that it works based on your ambitions alone.

The good news is that the modern age and smartphones have provided people with plenty more opportunities to get in control of their minds. From breathing to meditation and so much more, these smartphone apps will help you follow the techniques that we have discussed.

The problem is, sadly, that there are so many different options that you may not be sure which one is right for you. But you need to remember that many of these apps require that you pay some money, either via purchase or some sort of subscription. That is why you take great pains to make sure you only buy the one that is right for you.

Here are some of the best mindfulness apps that will help you get a better handle on your mind and the way it works, your breathing, your relaxation, your meditation and beyond. Please keep in mind that some of these apps work with certain smartphones and not with others.

Calm

An award-winning software called Calm offers breathing lessons and relaxation techniques. Even a Calm Kids component with meditations for children aged three to seventeen is included. You may know celebrities Matthew McConaughey and Jerome Flynn in one particular section, which offers a variety of vocal talents to help you drift off. There are additional breathing techniques, a mindful walking meditation, and relaxing activities for a mindful session you can enjoy directly from your Apple Watch.

Headspace

You may achieve peace and wellness, as well as balance by using Headspace's daily guided mindful breathing and meditation practices. Enjoy any of their brand-new sleep meditations, such as sleep casts with narrative, music, or natural soundscapes, prior to going to bed. You may learn the fundamentals of meditation and grow on them by using the app, which creates customized schedules depending on some input from you.

Breathe+

Regular breathing is not the same as breathing during meditation. If you want to feel in charge of your breathing while meditating and start to experience its effects, it may take some practice. This app's goal is to teach you how to breathe correctly so that you may experience the full advantages of meditative breathing, such as being able to maintain your breath for as long as thirty seconds and inhale or exhale even for little periods of time.

Buddhify

The buddhify app shows you how to handle difficult feelings, enhance your sleeping habits, and reduce stress with its several hundred meditations. Exercise awareness when doing activities that fit the category, such as driving, working, getting out of bed, eating, or even browsing the internet. Sessions can last anywhere from a few minutes to more than an hour, making this a viable alternative for both novice and seasoned practitioners.

The Mindfulness App

The Mindfulness App offers a wide range of alternatives for both novice and experienced meditators. You may begin with a five-day guided practice and introduction to mindfulness, and scheduled guided or solo meditation from three to thirty minutes to accommodate a hectic schedule. The app also provides customized meditation options, daily mindfulness notifications, and data to record in your meditation notebook.

Simple Habit

Daily meditation doesn't have to feel like a difficult habit to establish. This app provides a variety of 5-minute activities to assist you in developing a regular meditation practice. This app features a growing library of meditations for any moment of day, any scenario, and any objective.

Self-Talk

People with the issues you have often think pretty lowly of themselves. They often see themselves in a bad light, don't hold themselves in high regard, and give themselves an unhealthy dose of negative self-talk. This is only natural but it *must* be combatted if you really wish to change the way your brain works and declutter it too.

The truth is that everyone has multiple conversations every single day. Of course, we talk to coworkers, friends, family, loved ones, and even strangers on the street and people working at local stores. We talk to a lot of people every day, usually. It happens so much that we don't even think about it half of the time.

However, do you know the person you talk to the most during the day? Yourself. That's right, whether you know it or not, you are always having a conversation with yourself and it is often about yourself too. You talk to yourself, you encourage yourself, and you criticize yourself every hour of the day. You can be your biggest fan or your largest critic.

This is the definition of self-talk and it's a very big part of everyone's life and it's also something that will heavily impact your emotions, for better but often for worse too. Unfortunately, your self-talk might be quite negative because of the problems that you have with your mindset and the inability to clear your mind. Also unfortunately, you might not even be sure that you're doing this.

However, self-talk is something that we should all be aware of because it is very tricky and we often don't recognize that we are talking to ourselves. Therefore, we don't know what we are saying or the influence it has on our emotions, how we feel, and how we live our lives. For someone like us who is already trying to beat back the impulses of our brains, self-talk is just another thing that needs to be controlled.

We have all had days when we haven't liked how we look or we are unhappy with some work we have done or we have doubts about ourselves that we can't avoid. We tell ourselves that we look fat, that we are awkward or that we aren't doing a good job at work.

This is self-talk and, as you can tell, it's negative self-talk. It might not be a conversation that we are vocally participating in, but it's important just the same. We are talking to ourselves and by doing so we are furthering opinions about ourselves and what we can and can't do and what we are and aren't worthy of.

The most troublesome thing about self-talk is that the things we tell ourselves will only grow larger. They will snowball from just one small, stray thought into something that is much bigger - and much more dangerous too. It works like this: one day you tell yourself that you look overweight when you wear a certain shirt. Before you know it, just a short time later, you are telling yourself that you are always fat and that no outfit looks good on you.

Self-talk is something that can lead to being self-defeating. And it will lead from one thought to another. Following the example we have already addressed, you can see how it will soon spread to you feeling that you aren't worthy of love because you aren't attractive and no one will want to be with you.

This self-talk will then lead to you not believing in yourself and eventually not even trying to achieve much. And that will wind up with you feeling depressed, unworthy of love, and just not very special in any way at all.

Self-talk can greatly impact your emotions in some substantial ways. Perhaps one of the worst ways is that it can tell you that you shouldn't feel a certain way. Your self-talk might command you to avoid certain emotions or not feel a particular way. That will only lead to you bottling things up, avoiding them, and not really processing your emotions. If you want emotional regulation, it'll be very hard to achieve that if your negative self-talk is criticizing you for your emotions. Remember, there is nothing wrong with feeling things. If your self-talk behavior critiques you for feeling a certain way, it will create very bad emotional habits.

So, how do we change that? How do you make sure that your self-talk habits are positive and healthy and will make you feel better instead of worse? You shouldn't be your biggest critic, you should be your biggest cheerleader, your loudest and most steadfast and reliable supporter.

Of course, it's not just as easy as saying that you'll be more positive with the things you tell yourself but that really is a good place to start when you are attempting to improve your self-talk habits. You should be realistic about all situations you're in but you should make sure that you also focus on the positive. If you're going to partake in an important business meeting, you should start the day by telling yourself that you'll have something special and important to contribute. You should tell yourself that you're going to have a good day. You should remind yourself that you have the ability to help other people and create and foster meaningful relationships.

If you are ever in situations when you look back on how you acted and wished that things had gone differently, it is vital that you are pragmatic about the event. We all have a tendency to be very hard on ourselves but it is important that you don't focus solely on the negative. How do you do that? By looking at the situation and then coming up with ideas about how you would have handled things differently. What would you do if the very same situation presented itself? By doing this, you are going to instill belief in yourself, remain realistic about things, and put a plan into place so that you can ease your mind.

Get Good Sleep

It should go without saying that if you don't get good sleep, you won't feel well. We have all had those days when we feel like total trash, just dragging along, because we haven't achieved a lot of good rest.

We all need rest. Literally every single person alive needs some form of rest often or else they won't be able to function well. And this is especially true for people who are trying to have a better understanding of their emotions.

Yes, you need good, solid rest. This is a key way to ensure that you are awake, energetic in the right ways, and capable of getting through life and work with ease, no matter how troubling and crowded your brain can be at times.

Now, it is important to always remember that rest doesn't always mean curling up in bed and getting good sleep. Rest instead means getting quality downtime and time to allow your body and your mind to relax.

You need to do certain things like turn your brain off before you go to sleep. Don't start scrolling through TikTok, don't tend to your work assignment before you try to close your eyes or get sucked into a video game when you should be letting your mind and your body get some R&R.

If you don't let yourself rest, you are basically encouraging your mind to continue to spin for hours upon hours on end.

And what happens when that occurs?

We have all had periods in our lives when we haven't rested like we should. We feel sluggish, we feel out of sorts, and we may even make some serious mistakes. One of the most reliable ways to screw up at work is to not get good rest. Your brain simply cannot keep up with the tasks assigned to it if it hasn't been given proper and fulfilling rest.

Much like meditation, there are plenty of apps out there that will ensure you get a good night's sleep. But much of the responsibility will lie solely on you. You need to set a bedtime for yourself at night. That might feel like something that only little kids have to do but it's important that you allow your body and mind the time to get the rest it needs so much.

You should aim for eight hours of sleep a night but that's not always possible. Sometimes you'll get less than that, sometimes you'll get more. But here is one thing you should do: you should not be scrolling on your phone or watching TV during those eight hours. Create a routine for yourself that will encourage your body to rest, relax, and get some quality sleep.

It's also vital that you don't eat right before bed either. Not only will that be bad for your physical health - and can lead to weight gain and other health problems - but it will not allow you to get good sleep. The same is true for drinking alcohol. If you drink a lot right before sleep, you will wake up feeling groggy - or even worse. Far too many people are under the assumption that they'll get good sleep when they drink a lot but that isn't true. The opposite is true. You might sleep for a long time if you drink a lot but you will not be getting good sleep.

Resting gives your body and mind time to recharge, refresh and prepare for the next day and the jobs you'll need to finish. This means that your brain will be better primed for the new day and in a stronger condition. This will not ensure that your brain never acts out or becomes cluttered again but it will go a long way to making sure your mind is in the best state possible.

Rest will let your mind get some much needed R&R and that's a great and essential key to making sure that it's relaxed and healthy. That, of course, is the best way to have your mind ready to be maintained when it starts acting out or adding a bunch of worry and stress to your life again.

Now, you need to remember that rest doesn't always mean laying in bed with your eyes closed and dreaming, but it does mean getting off your feet, taking time to not do anything, and letting your body do what it naturally wants. And when you let your body do that, you are setting your brain up for success.

Nourish Your Mind, Body, And Soul

There are many people who turn to food when they aren't feeling great mentally. This is a creature comfort that most of us are familiar with. Whether it be your mom's home cooking, a certain drink that we love, or our favorite fast food chain, food can provide great comfort when we feel wiped out and anxious and not like our usual selves.

However, we all know people who spend too much time digging through their refrigerators when things aren't going their way. When their brains start acting out and start to get unruly, some people race to food and that is a very unhealthy habit that will actually make you unhappy.

Eating a poor diet is a quick way to feel even worse. Not only will your body suffer because of it, but your mental state will too. Filling your stomach with empty calories might make you feel better for a couple of minutes but soon after that, you'll crash from your sugar high in multiple ways. Your body will feel wiped out, your mind will also be fatigued, and your emotions will fall down a slippery slope too.

The good news is that there are certain foods that will not only take care of your body but also your mind and heart and soul too. If you are looking to clear your mind and continually soothe it, you might need to redirect your diet and change it.

If you're looking to boost your mood and make your mind feel better, here are some foods that you should add to your next shopping list. You will find that they help you control your emotions and generally feel better throughout the day. Eating food isn't just about nurturing the body, it's about nurturing the mind as well.

JAMES BROOK

Fatty Fish

You need to pay close attention to Omega-3 fatty acids when you are trying to improve your diet and your mental well-being. Your body cannot produce them on its own so you will need to turn to food.

Omega-3s are known to improve your mental state and lower your levels of depression. They add to the fluidity of the brain cell's membrane and also appear to have a key role in the development of the brain.

Do you like salmon? If so, you are in luck because it is packed with Omega-3s. A diet that includes this regularly will help your overall mood and will also assist you in controlling your emotions when you are having a bad day.

Dark Chocolate

That's right, chocolate can be good for you. Rejoice, because you have never heard news as good as this.

Yes, many forms of chocolate can just be empty calories and excess sugar. But that isn't always true with dark chocolate. It has been proven to improve your mood because of the mix of compounds inside of it, such as caffeine, theobromine, and N-acylethanolamine, which is actually chemically similar to cannabinoids.

Dark chocolate has also been shown to increase blood flow to your brain, reduce inflammation, and also boost your overall brain health. All of this can add to a better mood.

Of course, it is vital that you don't get carried away with your chocolate intake. Some people go overboard and they feast on chocolate. But that leads to them eating M&Ms, Reese's, and so much more. Delicious? Yes. Good for you? Not so much.

If you want the sort of chocolate that is good for your body and your mind, you need to stick to dark chocolate. The darker, the better. Additionally, even the healthy chocolate that we have spoken of should be enjoyed in moderation.

Bananas

Bananas are packed full of vitamin B6, which can synthesize neurotransmitters like serotonin and dopamine. It also comes with fiber. When sugar is paired up with fiber, it can slowly release into your body and give you stable blood sugar levels and will also provide you with better mood control. Some people even pack "emergency bananas" in their bags or purses because they know it can give them a boost of good energy during a tough day.

Oats

If you want to be in good spirits, starting your day off with some oats might help with that.

Oats are a whole grain that come in many forms. There are plenty of options for them when you go to the store. The thing that is so great about them is that they are a wonderful source of fiber and come with 8 grams in a single raw cup! Fiber is good because it helps you digest carbs and also releases sugar slowly into your bloodstream. This improves your energy levels which also improves your attitude and mood.

Studies have shown that people who enjoy a good amount of oats in the morning generally feel better about themselves, their work, their relationships, and their lives throughout the day.

Berries

Not only are berries so yummy and delicious, but they are also good for your mental health too. It's not entirely clear why but eating vegetables and fruits, such as berries, has been shown to lower rates of depression in study-takers.

Maybe it's because berries are filled with so many antioxidants and phenolic compounds, which help combat oxidative stress, which is an imbalance of harmful compounds residing in your body.

The tricky thing about adding berries to your diet is that so many companies sell "fake" berries that say they are authentic but actually are not. You need to focus on buying fresh, frozen berries and at peak ripeness if you want to enjoy all the antioxidants they have to offer.

Now it is time to cover the last part of our mental health journey. This last step, this final chapter, will be about therapeutic options to improve your mental well-being and your overall emotional state. This could perhaps be the best and most reliable way to make your mind feel better and give you a better mastery of your mind.

Exercising

If you have ever been out and about exercising, then you know how it feels when you're all done. You might feel a little tired, of course, but generally you feel great. In fact, you may have felt restless and tired before your exercise session but afterwards you felt completely revitalized.

The act of exercising has an ability to make you feel both better physically as well as mentally and that is one of the reasons why someone with a very cluttered and busy brain should put energy into working out. It doesn't have to be anything drastic - you don't have to end your sessions dripping in sweat. But exerting energy with exercise is a great way to make sure that you are healthy and happy and that your mind is in a good place.

There is verifiable scientific proof that says that this sort of movement will help your brain and will make it easier to sort through emotions, make goals, achieve them, and feel like you have peace of mind. There are many reasons for this and all of them are proven. These scientific studies have uncovered the fact that exercise that you experience regularly like walking or riding your bike or jogging can reduce certain depressive symptoms as well as "clear the mind". In fact, some studies have concluded that this sort of movement can be just as good for you as medication.

Many people think of exercising as a form of meditation, which is something we spoke of before. The power of meditation is crucial for people who have noisy minds. This sort of exercise will allow you to stay mindful, focus on the here and now, and not let your brain get carried away with the sort of thoughts that ultimately don't really matter.

If you feel like you are having a bad mental health day and your brain isn't listening to you, taking a long "mindfulness walk" might be perfect for you. This simply entails you getting outside and wandering for a while. You don't have to have a formal destination in mind and you also don't need to know how long you'll be walking for. Instead, you simply need to just get out there and get moving.

As you are walking, make sure that you pay attention to…just about everything. Take note of the color of the flowers that you see. You should also notice the smells of local barbecues or restaurants, the sounds of traffic in the distance, and the feeling of the wind on your face.

Every time you notice one of these things, be mindful of it. Use it as a reason to slow down a bit and soak it in. Try to not focus on other things. Instead, keep your mind centered around the feelings, the sounds and elements around you in the moment.

If you have more than simply a busy brain, exercising will do even more for you. Those suffering from ADHD and Bipolar Disorder have seen improved results when they get out every single day. It is important to remember that symptoms may return but generally these people experience at least 20 minutes of minimized symptoms. For those who suffer a lot of ADHD, Bipolar, and others, this can be a huge help.

Those who have a hard time focusing have found increased dedication to certain tasks and projects when they are regularly moving. Their motivation to follow through on these things is improved if they walk for about 20-30 minutes a day.

There are dozens of ways to move. Of course, walking is just one of them, so is cycling or jogging. But there are plenty more you can try if you want to experience the way that moving can quiet your mind or help it focus. Tai Chi, yoga, stretching, swimming, and even things as simple as jumping jacks can help.

Here are a few other surprising things about moving when it comes to your mental health. For one, it doesn't matter if you continually walk longer and longer, you will still be helping your mental health status. This isn't something where you will see diminished results if you are doing it regularly. You can add time to your walks or your jogs or your time at the yoga study and you won't build up a resistance. There are people who walk for more than an hour every single day and they are still getting so much from it.

It's also important to remember that you can do this with other people. In fact, there are many doctors who feel that walking or moving in pairs or in groups is actually even more beneficial to your mental health. Is this because you are also having a social event with your walks? We aren't entirely sure but this shows why you see so many couples and friends walking down the street at the end of the day. Not only is it good for them, it also makes them feel good too.

What is it about moving that makes you feel in control of your brain? It goes beyond the proteins that are fostered in your brain. There is a very deep reason why moving can make you feel better emotionally and why it can help quiet your mind.

It's no secret that people feel good once they get out and give themselves some much needed exercise. Yes, the proteins in your mind are part of it. And, yes, the Vitamin D that you will receive via your skin's exposure to sunshine will help too. But you will feel good also because you know you are doing something proactive to take care of your body. You will help your heart rate, your weight, your physical health and well-being, and so much more.

In so many ways, making sure that you move daily is a great way to not only take care of your body - and maybe shed a few pounds - but also help your mind be controlled by you. You will find that you are soon able to work through thoughts with ease, quiet the negative thinking that bogs you down, and just generally feel more optimistic.

And how much movement should you do every day if you are looking to regulate your emotions? Most doctors agree about 20 to 30 minutes every single day of rapid movement is important. This doesn't mean you need to be pouring with sweat or panting when you are all done, but you should try to get your heart beat moving a bit faster. You should feel as if you are moving a bit quickly, maybe breaking just a bit of a sweat, and feeling the elements like the sun and breeze around you.

The good news is that today there are a number of smart watches and apps for your phone that can keep track of all this. They can remind you to take a walk, do yoga, go jogging or do cardio and they can keep track of how much you move, how fast your heart moves, how many steps you take, and even how many calories you burn. Of course, the purpose behind this movement isn't about calories or weight loss, it's about making your mental health status brighter and more manageable. All of the other things that will come, are just added benefits.

Journaling

Yet another way for you to keep your mind quiet, even when it feels like that is impossible, is to get your thoughts together in the form of a diary or journal. To many, this is a lost art that can do such great things for you. For years, people have used journals, as a way to get a better grasp on what they were feeling, the problems they were facing, and how to overcome them all.

If you're someone who feels like you have a cluttered mind that never really goes silent, even after a long and stressful and busy day, then journaling might be right for you. In fact, studies have shown that keeping a journal can be a rewarding and beneficial practice for all people, especially those with a rowdy and busy brain that likes to create challenges and rarely quietens.

The key to journaling is that you are honest about what you write and you do so regularly. Remember, no one, but you will be reading this journal. That means that you can write down anything at all, no matter how intense or vulnerable or embarrassing it is. Even if you feel that you have a good understanding of what you're feeling or how certain events may have affected you, it is still wise for you to write about it in your journal. That's because putting your thoughts into words is a way to process what you are feeling, make sense of it, and even understand it better. Make writing in your journal a regular habit. Whether it's daily, a few times a week, or even once a week, consistency will help you get better at it over time.

Consistency is key but that requires that you choose a time that works best for you to sit down and write daily. This is the big step that will make journaling a daily habit that you always feel happy to do. You can do this in the morning right when you wake up, before bedtime when you are laying down, or during lunch breaks. The bottom line is that having a designated time will ensure that it is easier to build the journaling habit.

When you write, you need to make sure that you are focused and the other things out in the world aren't pulling you in every other direction. That means that you will have to find a quiet

THE QUIET OF MIND

and comfortable space where you can focus and reflect without distractions. You will be surprised by how challenging this step can be. You might think you live in a quiet place but you'll find that might not necessarily be true and you'll discover that when you first start trying to journal. Some people like to play ambient music or nature sounds while they journal while others want pure silence. You need to decide which works best for you and stick with it.

You might journal in a way that is wildly different from others but that's okay because there is no single right or wrong method to journaling. Certain journalers like to write freeform paragraphs without much structure, almost like poetry, while other people tend to employ bullet points or lists and write their journals as if they are putting together a game plan or to-do list. You might also attempt to use certain prompts or writing about specific themes or events. When it comes to prompts, you can find plenty online that will get your mind working and will stimulate you with questions.

Remember that your journal is a personal space only for you and no one else. Therefore, don't be scared to be very frank, honest, and open with your feelings and thoughts, as well as your experiences. Honesty often leads to a deeper sense of self-reflection that will then lead to personal growth too.

Some people get hung up on the little things when it comes to journaling but you should resist the urge to nitpick your work. Remember, your goal is to declutter your mind via your journal and you don't need perfect grammar or spelling when you are doing that. Therefore, don't stress out about your grammar, spelling, or whether your writing is good enough. This isn't going to be published or read by others. As mentioned, journaling is for you and only you, and it doesn't need to be 100% perfect without faults. The act of journaling is what's important, not the amount of errors within your words.

If you need to, you should try different writing techniques, such as gratitude journaling, stream-of-consciousness writing, or dream journaling.

Gratitude writing is when you jot down all of the things that you are thankful for. This will put you in a good headspace and make you feel happier, and will also help you communicate better with those who mean a lot to you.

Stream-of-consciousness journaling is something that most people don't have experience with, and it might feel somewhat weird at first. With this method, you simply let your mind go where it wants to, not holding it back or keeping it reigned in. Many stream-of-consciousness journal entries look a lot like poetry and that's okay. In fact, after you have written it, you might not even completely understand what you've just created. That's okay too! As mentioned before, the act of writing is what matters most. Just getting your thoughts out, in any form or fashion, is the part of the process that will heal and steady your mind.

Dream journaling is the practice of recording your dreams in a journal or diary. It involves writing down the details of your dreams, including the events, characters, emotions, and any other notable aspects you remember upon waking up. The goal of dream journaling is to capture and preserve the content of your dreams for later reflection and analysis.

Dreams can be fleeting and easily forgotten, even shortly after waking up. By keeping a dream journal, you create a written record that allows you to revisit your dreams and gain insights into your subconscious thoughts, feelings, and experiences.

Explore what resonates with you the most and craft your journaling experience based upon what you like and what you don't like. What feels good, what doesn't? Whatever works for you is what you should pursue, always remembering that as long as it is helping ease your mind, you are doing it correctly.

Periodically read through your past entries to see patterns, progress, and insights. Reflecting on your own thoughts can offer valuable perspectives. This will help you see the progress that you have made and will put things in perspective for you. You may be surprised by just how well-maintained and comfortable your brain is after even a few weeks of journaling. In the moment, it might not feel like you are doing much but, over time, you will notice a sizeable difference in how you are feeling day-to-day.

And if you feel like you have run out of ideas or things to talk about, you are in luck because there are many options out there that can help get your mind moving again and give you plenty of things to write about. If you ever feel stuck or don't know what to write about, use prompts to spark your creativity. There are countless journaling books as well as websites, apps, podcasts, and more that provide interesting prompts to get you started. A prompt typically comes in the form of a question or interesting premise that will get your mind thinking. They are a good place for you to start.

It is important that you keep your journal with you and accessible as much as possible. If you do this, you will be able to quickly write down your feelings any time you have a thought or feeling you want to capture. You can jot it down immediately and then quickly start processing what you're feeling.

Consider incorporating sketches, doodles, photos, or mementos into your journal. Adding visual elements can enhance the experience and make it more enjoyable. Since your journal is a place for your thoughts and feelings, you should feel free to bring anything that you create into it. Journaling doesn't have to be just about written words.

Some people expect to have a decluttered mind right away after they start journaling but that rarely is the case and it puts too much pressure on you. Therefore, always keep in mind that building your journal will take you some time, and that is totally normal. It's also normal and okay if you miss a few days here and there. You want to try to keep a strong, reliable schedule but things happen and people aren't 100% perfect. Give yourself some grace and don't be too hard on yourself. Always remember that the most important thing is to get back into it and keep going.

Missing a few days isn't a huge deal but it's also not an excuse to not pick up your journal again.

Remember, journaling is a personal journey, so find what works best for you and enjoy the process. Over time, you'll likely notice improvements in your writing, self-awareness, and overall satisfaction with keeping a journal.

The Benefits Of Journaling

Our book is about clearing your mind and being in control of it, even after years of feeling like that is impossible. Obviously, journaling is a great way to help with that. But, beyond that, journaling is great for you and your mental health for a variety of other reasons too, as it offers numerous mental, emotional, and even physical benefits.

Self-Reflection: Journaling provides a space for self-reflection and introspection and this is one of the biggest benefits that comes from it. When you write down all of your thoughts and experiences, you will get a better understanding of your emotions, your behaviors, and your patterns of thinking. Self-reflection is key to improving yourself and improving your mind so it's a super important part of journaling.

Stress Reduction: Everyone wants to feel calm, especially those of us with cluttered and loud noises. And writing in your journal will end up being a form of emotional release for you, which will help you reduce your stress and anxiety levels. Expressing emotions in your book might assist you in processing any challenging emotions as well as coping with daily stressors that can add to an already-crowded brain.

Improved Emotional Intelligence: Regular journaling can enhance emotional intelligence by deepening your understanding of your own emotions and also how they often influence the thoughts and actions you undertake in your day-to-day life.

Emotional intelligence, also known as EI, basically refers to an ability to see, comprehend, manage, and then express all of your emotions effectively. It also incorporates your ability to understand and communicate with other peoples' emotions too. EI involves a grouping of skills which allows people to get through their emotions and all social interactions in a strong, smart, healthy, and constructive manner. Because of that, it is an important part of personal and social development, and will impact certain aspects of your life, like your relationships, decision-making skills, and overall well-being.

Emotional intelligence is not fixed, which means that it can be grown, enhanced, and improved with practice, self-awareness, as well as hard work. People with higher emotional intelligence levels tend to have better interpersonal relationships with others, they also exhibit more effective leadership qualities, and experience improved overall well-being. It is a valuable skill set in various settings, including personal life, the workplace, and social interactions.

Enhanced Creativity: Beyond your emotional intelligence and peace of mind, keeping a journal encourages creativity, as it allows you to explore ideas and thoughts freely. Engaging in creative writing can stimulate the imagination and problem-solving abilities.

Being creative is a great way to solve problems, although some people don't necessarily realize that. When you enhance your creative mind, you will find ways to think outside of the box and solve things in new ways. Whether it be money problems or relationship issues, if you improve the creative side of your cluttered mind, you will find solutions that didn't seem possible before.

Working on a journal regularly is one of the smartest and best ways to make sure that the creative part of you is not only surviving but actually thriving.

Goal Setting and Achievement: Journaling helps you set and track goals, making them more tangible and achievable. It provides a record of your progress and motivates you to stay focused on your objectives.

Goal setting is incredibly important for all types of people but especially those who often suffer with a cluttered mind. That is because a mind that is busy and cluttered and full of unnecessary things will make it hard for you to stay on task and get things done like they need to be. You can easily be distracted and pulled away in multiple directions at one time. Therefore, creating some serious goals and doing whatever is necessary to reach them is a great way to help your mind stay in line.

Memory Improvement: Another thing that people with cluttered minds suffer from is a bad memory. Because your brain is seemingly so full of content, most of it unneeded, you might not always hold onto every thought like you want to. They might slip through your fingers like sand at the beach.

But writing about the experiences in your daily life in a journal will help keep these memories and can also improve the ability to hold onto details and important events too. Overall, this will enhance your memory and make you able to recall things more often, even if you have struggled with this in the past.

This might not seem like something that is very helpful but it can actually be a huge boost to someone with a cluttered mind. Why? Because many times, our minds are working overtime to try to remember things, like when your appointment is or where you left your keys. With a stronger sense of memory, that won't be nearly as big an issue and that will result in your brain being calmer and able to focus on other things.

Positive Thinking: Practising gratitude journaling can foster a more positive outlook on life. By focusing on the things you are grateful for, you can shift your attention away from negativity and by writing down the things that you want to change, you can start to build a very reasonable, reliable and steadfast plan that you will follow to improve your life. This too will create more positive thinking and a strong outlook on yourself and what you are doing.

Positive thinking will lead to more self-belief too. That will help you in the future as well and you will find that you are soon your biggest fan and cheerleader and you'll feel capable of believing in yourself.

Improved Communication Skills: Journaling can serve as a practice ground for expressing yourself more effectively which can improve your communication skills in daily life. When you starting putting your thoughts to words regularly, you will then begin to speak more confidently, more openly and more accurately with others too, no matter what you are talking about.

Self-Awareness and Personal Growth: Regularly recording your thoughts and experiences allows you to track personal growth over time and identify areas for self-improvement.

This is great for you because it'll keep you on track and allow you to complete your tasks and reach your goals. But it is also good for you because it'll give you ample evidence of your ability to complete things, stick to tasks and be productive.

Many people who have cluttered and loud brains sadly, also have low self-esteem and a bad self-image at times. We regularly feel bad about ourselves because we notice we're continually coming up short, not achieving what we want, and not being as proactive as we'd like.

When you are able to journal regularly, you will also be able to be more self-aware and honest about the personal growth you have undergone. This will give you a boost of energy and belief in yourself and will help you in the long run, no matter what goals are at hand.

Problem Solving: Journaling can help you analyze and work through problems, providing a structured approach to finding solutions.

Think of writing in a journal like doing a math problem. You will write out the issue at hand and what you want to achieve. By doing that, you will also start to figure out solutions for yourself too. Writing out your problems will regularly help you find solutions and keeping up with your journal won't only help ease and calm your mind, it'll also enhance your problem-solving abilities.

Health Benefits: Did you know that writing in a journal is literally good for your body? It's true! Studies have shown that regular journaling might have serious and testable physical health benefits, like reducing symptoms of some conditions such as asthma and even arthritis. Meanwhile, others have discovered that journaling allows people to rest much better and deeper for a longer time. Additionally, some people have found that they suffered from fewer panic attacks and anxiety problems throughout the day when they are regularly journaling.

Catharsis: Writing about difficult or traumatic experiences can offer a sense of catharsis, allowing you to release pent-up emotions and find closure. When you write down what you are feeling, you are actively processing it all and letting it go. This will lift a very heavy weight off your shoulders and will make you feel free from some of the suffocating feelings that you have.

Better Decision Making: Journaling can help you clarify your thoughts and make more informed decisions by weighing pros and cons on paper.

As mentioned before, when you actually write out a situation or a problem at hand, you can usually wrap your mind around it in a better way. It makes it easier to grasp, easier to comprehend, and easier to solve.

The more you journal, the more you will find that it is easier to make decisions that are better for you. People who regularly journal about their days often eventually find that they are capable of making snap decisions that are healthy and smart.

In total, journaling is a valuable tool for self-discovery, self-improvement, and overall well-being. It's a versatile practice that can be adapted to suit individual preferences and needs, making it a powerful tool for personal growth and development.

For those of us who have cluttered minds that rarely turn off, journaling is a way to sort through all of the noises presented to us all day long. Journaling is a way to slow down, take a look at what we are feeling, and begin to process emotions, make plans, and better ourselves. It's a way to tell our story to ourselves, see what we want to change and what we do well. It's a great way to improve ourselves and our lives and also free our brains from some of the unnecessary baggage that we carry around all the time.

To-Do Lists & Calendars

Everyone needs reminders at certain times in their lives. Sometimes, they need reminders to pay their rent and maybe they need reminders to make a phone call to family or friends. Others need reminders to buy groceries, do household chores, and more. There is nothing wrong with creating reminders and to-do-lists and using calendars for yourself.

And people with cluttered minds need them more than others. That is because the busy brains that we have make it much harder to keep track of things, even mandatory tasks and errands that need to be finished. But the good news is that we have plenty of ways to create to-do lists and calendars. Now more than ever before, we have the power to remind ourselves of just about anything - all from the power of our smartphones.

A to-do list can ease your mind, no matter how busy it gets, in many ways. Let's discuss why creating these lists and using calendars and relying on simple reminders will make your life much easier, even when your brain is pushing back against you in a big way.

First and foremost, creating and maintaining a regular to-do list will assist you in organizing your tasks, errands, responsibilities, as well as thoughts. When everything you need to do in the day or the week is plainly written down for you in an app or even on a piece of paper, it goes a long way to reducing the mental clutter in your mind and also provides some serious clarity about what has to be done - and when.

The alternative is just too much of a mess, and you're well aware of that. Throughout the years, you have found that when your tasks and responsibilities float around without much structure in your mind, it creates a massive amount of panic and anxiety. Writing all of these tasks down in a list takes that burden that is weighing your mind down and puts it on paper. This provides a sense of relief because you are able to easily and regularly see what needs to be done.

Of course, you need to ensure that the list you are making is truly comprehensive. You can't miss out on things and you can't forget even the simplest, smallest tasks. A well-structured list will allow you to prioritize your tasks depending on their level of importance and the deadlines tied to them. This assists your focus on the most critical tasks first, making you more productive and less overwhelmed. Of course, it might take you some time to really formulate the right to-do list that you will need to follow day-in and day-out. And, frankly, the creation of that list might feel a bit overwhelming at the moment. But remind yourself that it will all work out for the best and will help you in the long run. It's worth it because once you are done creating your to-do list, it'll make your life so much easier and you will be able to use it daily.

For those of us who sometimes feel like our brains are out of control, finishing items on a to-do list feels incredible and like a huge accomplishment. Checking off these completed errands on your list will provide you with a sense of true accomplishment as well as a feeling of accountability too. All in all, it provides a positive reinforcement for you and also motivates you to keep it up. We mentioned positive reinforcement before and finishing something on your to-do list is one of the biggest examples of it.

With a to-do list, you will not have to fret about possibly forgetting some of the important tasks in your day or that you have appointments. It will serve as a reliable memory aid.

By planning your day or week ahead with a to-do list, you can allocate time more efficiently and avoid wasting time. You will be able to do so many other things instead of planning your day. From hanging out with friends, to leisure time and to work efforts, you will be capable of accomplishing so much more because your to-do list will keep you in line, give you peace of mind, and assure you that certain things won't slip through the cracks.

Essentially, this list performs as a map for your day-to-day life, making sure that you keep on track and remain focused, at all times. This will improve your productivity levels and prevent procrastination. Procrastination is one of the biggest opponents for people with cluttered minds. It can get the better of you, even if you are trying hard to avoid it.

It will also go a long way to making sure you have a thriving personal life as well as a great job too. When you have a to-do list, you will be able to make boundaries that sit between your work and your personal life. You can make a formative to-do list related to your job and when you have finished everything on it, you know it's time to unwind and relax.

When your mind is filled with worries about tasks you need to complete, it can interfere with your sleep. That is why some people advise that you write down and add to your to-do list right before your bedtime so you can help keep your mind clear. This, of course, will make it easier to fall asleep and that will also go a long way to making sure your mind is less cluttered.

And you shouldn't ever think you need to be too beholden to the list that you make. You can always change it if you need to. One of the great things about to-do lists is that they can be easily adjusted as your circumstances change over time. This will obviously give you the flexibility to accommodate new tasks or changes in priorities. Don't be afraid of changing your list if you need to, just be sure that you always stick to the list that you settle upon. Don't let changes to it be an excuse to not follow it closely.

Knowing that you have a plan in place for the day or week gives you a sense of control over your life and reduces the feeling of being overwhelmed.

Overall, a to-do list acts as a valuable tool to organize your life, manage stress, and enhance productivity. It allows you to offload mental burdens, make progress on your goals, and experience a greater sense of peace of mind.

Pursuing Hobbies

Sometimes the act of clearing your mind and finding your inner peace might feel like a challenge and, sometimes, it might feel like a lot of work too. But that doesn't always have to be the case. In fact, believe it or not, sometimes clearing your mind can be fun. That is because if you have some hobbies that you truly love and enjoy doing, you can use them as a tool to declutter your brain and quiet your mind.

Engaging in hobbies has been proven to be a wonderful way to help clear your mind, reduce your stress levels, and also promote your relaxation. There are many hobbies that are known to help people achieve a clearer and more peaceful state of mind. Have you ever practiced any of these hobbies?

Yoga: Nearly everyone who is passionate about yoga says just how good it is for both their body and their mind. Yoga combines physical postures with breath control and mindfulness, promoting relaxation, flexibility, and mental clarity. Many of the techniques that we have talked about when it comes to relaxation are put into practice doing yoga poses, which proves just how great it can be for clearing your cluttered mind.

Reading: Immersing yourself in a good book can transport your mind to a different world, providing a mental escape from stressors and worries. If you're lucky, you have had experiences, whilst reading, where you get lost in the pages and the world that is built by the author. It's a great way to clear your mind and forget about your worries. And it also has a physical contribution too. Your breathing will slow, you will feel more peace and relaxation, and you can also get some good sleep if you need too. Many people spend the last hour before bed as a time to read because of the way it benefits their mindset and gets them ready for a great night of rest.

Drawing or Painting: Are you someone who is talented when it comes to pens, pencils, or paintbrushes? If so, you might have a hobby that can lead the way to a quiet mind. Engaging in creative activities such as drawing, painting, or coloring can help you focus your mind on the artistic process and create a sense of calm. Not only will you feel better when it's done, but you'll also have a wonderful piece of artwork to hang on the wall or give to someone else too.

Playing a Musical Instrument: Playing an instrument requires concentration and engagement, which can help shift your focus away from stressors and into the music. When you are performing, whether it be at home, at an open mic, or among friends and peers, you will have to focus your concentration on playing your instrument. That means that your mind will have to do away with all of the excessive thoughts that bog it down usually. It's a great relief from the stress of your brain, even if it's just temporary.

Gardening: Getting outdoors and being at one with nature is a terrific way to get some sun, be productive, and calm your mind.

Working with plants and being in a garden can have a soothing effect on the mind. Gardening allows you to engage in a hands-on activity while enjoying the outdoors. Plus, it will expose you to sunshine, which will boost your vitamin D levels. That is the vitamin that has been proven to improve your mood. Just make sure you load up on the sunscreen!

Cooking or Baking: Do you want to help your mind find peace and also fill your tummy with delicious food? You're in luck because preparing meals or trying out new recipes can be a mindful activity that engages your senses and allows you to focus on the present moment.

Knitting or Crocheting: Much like painting or drawing, knitting and crocheting are rhythmic activities that can have a calming effect and help you clear your mind. And, like playing an instrument, they force your brain to focus solely on the task at hand and nothing else, prohibiting it from wandering and becoming cluttered.

Hiking or Nature Walks: Spending time in nature and going for a hike or a leisurely walk can provide a break from urban noise and help you connect with the natural world. Much like spending time in the garden is good for you, so are nature walks and hiking outdoors. It's a form of exercise and it's also a way to get mindful, soak in the environment around you, and disassociate from the worries and distractions in your busy brain.

Photography: Exploring your surroundings through the lens of a camera can encourage you to notice details and beauty that you might otherwise overlook.

Puzzles and Brain Teasers: Engaging in puzzles, crosswords, Sudoku, or other brain-teasing games can divert your focus from stressors and challenge your mind in a different way. Some people with cluttered minds have found that they are actually quite good at these types of puzzles because their brains are capable of thinking outside the box.

Writing or Journaling: As we have mentioned before, expressing your thoughts and emotions through writing in a journal or diary can help you gain clarity and perspective on your feelings. It can help you process what you are feeling, put it behind you, make plans for yourself in the future, and also decompress and calm down.

Volunteering: Helping others and engaging in acts of kindness can bring a sense of purpose and fulfillment, which can contribute to a clearer state of mind. You will not only feel better mentally but you will feel better emotionally too and you'll be proud of yourself and happy with the ways that you are helping other people.

DIY Projects: Engaging in do-it-yourself (DIY) projects or crafts allows you to channel your creativity and focus on the task at hand. Much like crocheting, knitting, painting, or any type of art, you will have a result from all your work too and that'll make you feel happy and also proud of your accomplishments.

In the end, the best hobby for you to clear your mind will depend upon your personal preferences and interests. Think of what makes you happiest and what you're best at. You may have gone through your life not knowing that the hobbies you have can help clear your mind, but they can. You just need to approach them from a different angle and think of them in a new way.

The most important thing is that you choose pastimes that allow you to be fully present, engage your senses, and provide a sense of enjoyment and relaxation.

Seeking Help

There may come a point when you feel that you just cannot do this on your own. The concept of quieting your mind and finding inner peace might just feel like its too much, too overwhelming or too daunting. You may fear that it is impossible, even after multiple attempts. You have meditated, you have breathed, you have worked so hard to find calm in the storms of your mind and nothing seems to be working.

But that doesn't mean it's impossible. It just means you might need help from someone else. And that is totally okay and acceptable. It is a very smart move for many, and it might be perfect for you.

In fact, finding a therapist can be an important step in taking care of your mental and emotional well-being as you venture on your journey to having a clear and peaceful mind. But it's not always an easy process and it requires some work.

Before you start your search, take some time to reflect on your specific needs and preferences. Consider the type of therapy you're looking for. For a busy and loud mind, you will want someone who can specialize and really help with things like anxiety, panic attacks and paranoia. Thankfully, there are many therapists and counselors who are well-suited to take care of your needs in that way. Also consider many other things, such as any preferences you have for the therapist's gender, age, cultural background, or therapeutic approach.

Remember, this is someone who you are going to really open up to and discuss many personal things with. It should be someone you are comfortable with in every single way.

At this point in your search for a therapist, you should treat this like a job interview. Only *you* are the person with the questions who is sizing up your potential matches. You will know when you finally settle upon who you want to help you when they check every box that you have and they feel like the perfect fit.

Researching local therapists in your area is vital when you are doing this search. There are several ways to research potential therapists. For example, many online directories list therapists along with their specialties, credentials, and contact information. Examples include Psychology Today, TherapyDen, GoodTherapy, and NetworkTherapy, and others. And any time you type in a therapist search into Google or your chosen search engine, you should get results for professionals near you.

Of course, you can also take the advice of people you know whose opinions you trust. To do this, just ask friends, family members, or healthcare professionals for recommendations. Nowadays, many people you know might be in some sort of counseling and therapy and they will be able to give you their own personal opinions on who they like and don't like. This is even more helpful because your friends and family know you better than anyone. Therefore, they likely know what will work and not work for you, they'll also know what sort of personalities and styles won't fit. Because of that, referrals like this can often provide valuable insights into a therapist's effectiveness and compatibility.

Therapy isn't free, even if it's very much needed. Hopefully, you won't have to pay out of pocket for your sessions but that is only possible if you have insurance. If you do, your insurance provider's website may have a list of therapists who accept your insurance. If you lack insurance, there are still options for you. Thankfully, many therapists also employ a sliding scale payments schedule with their clients, meaning you might not have to pay all at once each time you have an appointment, you may be able to create some sort of arrangement that works best for the budget that you have.

Although you can talk to your friends and family and get suggestions from them, you can also reach out to local mental health organizations or community clinics to inquire about available therapists.

When you have heard of a doctor that might feel like a good fit for you, you should then read reviews or testimonials from current or former clients. While individual experiences can vary, reviews can provide insights into a therapist's approach and effectiveness.

After that, reach out to the therapists you're interested in. You can call or email them to inquire about their availability, approach to therapy and fees. When you do, don't hesitate to ask questions about their experience, therapeutic approach, treatment methods, and what to expect during sessions. This can help you assess whether their approach aligns with your needs.

This would be the right time to inquire about session frequency, duration, fees, payment options, and cancellation policies. Make sure you understand the logistics before committing to therapy.

Finding a therapist you feel comfortable with is crucial. You should feel a sense of rapport and trust with your therapist. If you're not comfortable during the initial contact, it's okay to continue your search.

It's a good idea to consult with multiple therapists before making a decision. This allows you to compare their approaches and determine which one feels like the best fit for you.

Ultimately, trust your instincts when choosing a therapist. If you feel a positive connection and believe the therapist can help you, it's a sign that you're on the right track.

JAMES BROOK

Remember that finding the right therapist might take some time and effort, but investing in your mental health and well-being is worth it. Therapy can be a valuable tool for you as you attempt to find ways to quiet your mind and keep it under control, despite years of it speaking back to you and not letting you have your way.

Conclusion

Clearing your mind is really the biggest goal people think of when they discuss "decluttering" and that is why we have spent so much time and so many pages talking about it. This is really the core of decluttering your mind.

Thankfully, as you can see, there are many ways for you to do this. From just the simple act of spending a few minutes listening and tracking your breathing to more intense exercises like meditation, working out, and more, there are many ways for you to take matters into your own hands and find a way to quiet your brain.

It is important to remember a few things about this entire process. Firstly, and most importantly, it is going to take time and you need to give yourself both patience and grace. No matter which avenue you choose from the ones we have gone over, none of them will have overnight success. The vast majority of them need days and days, sometimes weeks or even months, of practice before you are going to notice something different. Even the process of finding a therapist isn't always quick and often requires some trial and error and hard work.

That might sound a bit frustrating because you have gone years with your cluttered mind and the problems that it brings. That means you don't want to wait any longer and you want results as soon as possible. They will come, but they might not come quickly.

When you are feeling the frustration about that, it's vital that you remind yourself that you *are* doing good and important work and you *are* making progress, even when it doesn't feel like it. And you need to always remember that you can't stop trying, even if it feels like you're spinning your wheels. Yes, you have spent years dealing with the issues of a cluttered brain. That is precisely why it isn't going to change overnight and you need to expect to work on these things often to accomplish what you want.

You have gone this long dealing with these problems but they could be behind you as long as you stay adamant and keep working hard and take this seriously. Help is coming, if you do what is necessary to take the first step.

CHAPTER 4

What Are Your Goals?

If you want to have a mind that is sustainably decluttered at all times, it is very important that you know what your goals are. This is true for all people but those of us with a busy brain often need to put more time and effort and energy into figuring out our goals and what we hope to accomplish. Why? Because it is sometimes harder for people like us to actually know when we have achieved these things. There is a chance that you could actually accomplish your goal without ever knowing it, or celebrating it.

When you have a goal, you can create a pathway to get there. But if you don't know your goal, you will wander aimlessly through life. To that end, having goals is important because they provide direction, motivation, focus, and a sense of purpose to our lives. And for those of us with cluttered minds, figuring them out will help us know we are on the right path and also keep track of the progress we have made.

Goals help provide a clear sense of direction and purpose. They give you a target to aim for and guide your actions and decisions. Without goals, you might feel lost or unsure about where you're headed. Additionally, they always serve as a source of motivation. When you have a specific goal in mind, you're more likely to stay motivated and work towards achieving it. The desire to accomplish something meaningful can drive you to take consistent and purposeful actions.

Setting goals helps you prioritize and focus your efforts and that's doubly important for those of us with busy brains. Finding focus can be difficult with so much noise in our heads but a well thought-out and substantial goal can give it to us. With a defined goal, you can avoid distractions and concentrate on tasks that contribute to your desired outcome, making you more productive and efficient.

Goals provide a way to measure your progress and success. They give you a framework to assess how far you've come and how much further you need to go. Tracking your progress can boost your confidence and provide a sense of accomplishment.

Pursuing goals often requires you to step outside your comfort zone, learn new skills, and overcome challenges. This process of growth and development can lead to increased self-confidence, resilience, and a broader range of abilities.

Goals help you manage your time effectively. When you have a goal in mind, you can allocate your time and resources efficiently to ensure that you're making steady progress toward achieving it.

Goals provide a framework for decision-making. If your brain is going a mile a minute, writing out and recognizing your goals will help you stay on track. When you are faced with choices, you can assess whether they align with your goals and make decisions that support your long-term aspirations.

Perhaps one of the most important things about goals is that you get a wonderful feeling of accomplishment when you achieve them. This positive feeling can boost your self-esteem and overall well-being.

Working towards and achieving meaningful goals can lead to a greater sense of happiness and fulfillment. When you're actively engaged in pursuing something you value, it adds a sense of purpose and joy to your life.

Having goals can make you more resilient in the face of setbacks and challenges. When you encounter obstacles, your commitment to your goals can help you persevere and find alternative solutions. And when you share your goals with others it can foster social interaction and support. Friends, family, or colleagues can provide encouragement, advice, and accountability as you work towards your goals.

Setting and pursuing goals is important because they provide direction, motivation, focus, and a sense of purpose. They empower you to take control of your life, grow as an individual, and experience a greater sense of accomplishment and fulfillment.

How Do You Figure Out Your Goals?

So, you know that having goals is an important part of silencing your mind and getting your life headed in the direction that you want. But how do you know what your goals are? That might sound like a silly question, but think about it: it is sometimes very hard for you to know what your goals are. There are big, overarching goals that we all have like "live a good life" and "make enough money to get by" but there are a bunch of mini-goals within those bigger ones that must be achieved.

Figuring out your goals is paramount to achieving them. So, creating a list of goals is also very important. It involves a structured process to ensure that your objectives are clear, achievable, and aligned with your aspirations and values.

Before you do anything, you need to take some time to reflect on various areas of your life, such as career, education, relationships, health, personal growth, and hobbies. Consider what you want to achieve in each area and what matters most to you. Think about both short-term and long-term goals.

When you start to get an idea of the goals that you want, make them all as specific and detailed as possible. Avoid vague or general statements like the ones that we just talked about. For example, instead of "get healthy," specify "lose 15 pounds by winter" or something that is more focused than that. Now is not the time to be abstract or vague.

Think of it this way: you want to know when you have achieved your goals. And you can't always know unless there is a definitive and reliable way to qualify it.

You will also have to make some tough choices at this point when you are creating your goals. That means you will have to determine when you want to be done with your accomplishment. Therefore, you have to set a deadline for achieving what you want. This is vital because it adds a sense of urgency and helps you stay focused.

In the course of figuring out what you want to achieve, you may find that there are quite a lot of things that you want to do. There is nothing wrong with that but you'll have to narrow your list and set a priority order for all of your many goals. Determine the importance and urgency of each goal you have in your life. Rank them all in order of priority so you can focus your efforts on the most critical objectives first.

Make it easier on yourself by seeing which goals are similar, which can be accomplished together, and what order you should go about doing it all. Do this by grouping similar goals together into smaller, more attainable categories. This can help you organize your list and see the bigger picture of your aspirations and it can also make sure you don't feel overwhelmed with the tasks at hand. Remember, we are trying to make sure your mind remains quiet now that you have found ways to calm it. Loading too much onto your plate at one time is a recipe for disaster.

Breaking things down is always a good idea when a task seems too big. If you have larger goals, break them down into smaller, manageable steps or milestones. This makes the goals less overwhelming and easier to tackle. You will see that if everything is assembled in a smaller, step-by-step, bite-sized process, it's all much more attainable.

Perhaps the most important thing you can do, especially since you suffer from a cluttered mind, is take the time to write your goals down. This solidifies your commitment and increases the likelihood that you'll stay focused on achieving them. It will also make everything feel much more achievable. When you have written everything down, you'll see that what you're attempting to achieve isn't nearly as big as you once thought.

Writing it all down will also allow you to take a good, deep look at your goals and figure out if you need to revise anything. You should regularly review your list of goals to track your progress and make any necessary adjustments. Life circumstances and priorities can change, so be open to revising your goals as needed. Plus, as time goes on, you might find that what was once your goal no longer is. There is nothing wrong with that and you need to be sure that if you make a discovery like it, you will plan accordingly and change it up.

Keep your goals visible and remind yourself regularly why you're working towards them. This can help maintain your motivation and enthusiasm. And, again, if you find that the reason why you're doing things has changed, it is alright if you decide that one goal is no longer as important as it once was.

You need people to tell you how well you are doing and the progress you are making. That is why you should share your goals with a friend, family member, or a mentor who can provide encouragement and hold you accountable for your progress. With them, celebrate your successes, no matter how small. Acknowledging your accomplishments boosts your confidence and keeps you motivated.

Goal-setting is a dynamic process. As you achieve goals or as circumstances change, your list of goals may evolve. Regularly review and adjust your goals to ensure they continue to reflect your aspirations and priorities.

Keep Progress Of Your Goals

Having goals is important and now that you have gone to great lengths to get a handle on your mind and keep it under control, your ability to achieve them - or at least make serious progress with them - is stronger than ever.

However, an important part of reaching your goals is being honest with yourself about what you have got done. It's vital that you often take a look at what you've achieved and how far you've come, as well as how far you still have to go.

JAMES BROOK

It is sometimes hard to really understand what you have accomplished when it comes to your goals. That means you might need to get creative. Knowing the type of mind you have, a creative approach to determining how much success you have had with your goals is a very smart idea.

For example, imagine your goals as stepping stones across a river. Each goal represents a distinct stone that you need to step on to reach the other side, where your achievements await. As you move forward, consider several strategies to keep track of your progress.

Riverbank Reflection:
Take a moment to sit on the riverbank and reflect on your goals. Visualize each stone and its significance. Ask yourself which goals are closer to the starting point and which ones are further along. This mental map helps you assess your progress intuitively.

Pebbles:
Collect small pebbles or stones to represent your goals. Place these pebbles in a visible location, such as a jar or bowl. As you make progress on a goal, move its corresponding pebble to a separate container. Watching the pebbles accumulate is a tangible reminder of your achievements.

Journey Journal:
Imagine your goals as chapters in a journal. Create a personal narrative for each goal, detailing your aspirations, steps taken, challenges faced, and milestones achieved. This journal serves as a story of your journey, allowing you to see how far you've come.

Vision Board:
Envision a wall covered with images, symbols, and words representing your goals. As you make progress, add visual cues that represent your achievements. Over time, this dynamic collage becomes a visual record of your advancement.

Puzzle Pieces:
Imagine your goals as puzzle pieces forming a complete picture of your aspirations. Each time you make progress on a goal, fit a corresponding puzzle piece into the larger picture. Watching the puzzle come together symbolizes your overall progress.

Nature Walk:
Picture your goals as trees in a forest. Walk through this metaphorical forest and observe the growth of each goal-tree. Notice which goals have strong branches (progress) and which ones need more nurturing. This imaginative stroll helps you evaluate your journey.

Musical Melodies:
Consider each goal as a note in a song. As you make progress, imagine playing each note more skillfully and harmoniously. Over time, the symphony of your achievements becomes a testament to your efforts.

Constellation Chart:
Picture your goals as stars in a night sky. Create a constellation chart by connecting the stars you've reached. Over time, this

celestial representation showcases your journey through the night toward your desired destination.

Recipe of Accomplishments:
Visualize your goals as ingredients in a recipe for success. As you make progress, add each accomplished goal as a key ingredient. Over time, you'll see the transformation of your endeavors into a fulfilling outcome.

Inner Compass:
Imagine your goals as points on a compass, guiding you toward your true north. Regularly assess your alignment with these points, making adjustments as needed to ensure you stay on course toward your desired destination.

By using these imaginative approaches, you can keep track of your goals in a creative and engaging way, allowing you to celebrate your progress and stay motivated on your journey of achievement.

The Benefits Of Meeting Your Goals

There is one clear benefit of meeting your goals: you get them done. It doesn't matter if it's receiving your drivers' license or buying a home or getting a new job, actually doing what you set out to do is one of the best things about success.

But meeting your goals can have a wide range of other positive features and benefits too, especially for people who have cluttered minds and, therefore, often have a difficult time achieving their goals.

Firstly, and perhaps most importantly, successfully achieving your goals provides a strong sense of accomplishment and satisfaction. It just feels good. No matter how much success you have had, there have been times in your life when you've met your goals and you know just how victorious you feel. Completion of your task or goal reinforces the idea that hard work, determination, and focus can lead to tangible results. There are few bigger boosts to your ego and your mental well-being than completing a goal.

Since your mind is often very loud, achieving your goals will feel even better than it does for most people. This is because, sadly, there have been many times in your life when something you want to do, even something simple, feels out of reach and hard to achieve. Your brain gets busy, you get distracted, you can't formulate a plan or you don't have confidence in yourself. All of this adds up to preventing you from getting what you want done.

Therefore, when you *do* achieve your goals, despite your cluttered mind, it feels even better and the pat on the back that you will get should be even bigger.

To that end, achieving your goals boosts self-confidence and self-esteem. It demonstrates your abilities and capabilities, which can positively impact how you perceive yourself and your potential. You will have more faith in yourself. The next time there is something that you need to accomplish, you'll believe that you can. It won't just be based on pure optimism. Every time you succeed and complete a goal you are giving yourself proof for the future that it can be done again.

It also might encourage you to do even more, try even harder, and get other things done. Accomplishing one goal can serve as motivation to pursue additional goals. Success breeds success, and achieving one goal can create a positive momentum that drives you to strive for more.

Meeting the goals that you have created for yourself also helps you track and then measure your progress and your growth. It creates a clear indicator of just how far you've come and what you've accomplished, which can be especially gratifying when looking back on your journey.

The attributes and personality features that you want to build and grow will only get stronger the more times that you succeed at meeting your goals. Setting and achieving these goals for yourself requires focus, discipline, and effective time management. Then, meeting your goals will help you develop and strengthen these valuable skills, which can be applied to other areas of your life.

You will also have a better sense of being able to overcome adversities when you achieve your goals. That is because working toward a goal usually involves overcoming obstacles as well as challenges. Therefore, successfully navigating these hurdles can improve your problem-solving skills and adaptability and your realization that you can be cool under pressure, composed, and able to make a plan and get things done.

The process of pursuing and achieving goals can build resilience and the ability to handle setbacks. Learning to persevere through challenges and setbacks can make you more resilient in the face of future difficulties.

The more that you complete your tasks and meet your goals, the better you will feel in every part of your life. You will find that achieving the goals you create for yourself will contribute to your overall well-being and happiness. The satisfaction that comes from meeting your goals can lead to improved mental and emotional health. It doesn't matter if you've completed a work goal or a home goal, the entirety of your life will feel better and happier because you have proven to yourself that you can overcome challenges, including the mental ones that your brain presents. You will also look better in the eyes of other people, which can help your relationships.

Accomplishments are often recognized and acknowledged by people close to you, which provides you with a sense of validation and external affirmation. This recognition can boost your confidence and reinforce your efforts. It can also make you feel closer to others. Additionally, your value with other people might also rise too and they could see you as a hard worker or someone reliable.

Perhaps the best thing about meeting your goals is that it will push you and make you achieve more and grow as a person. Meeting these goals usually involves discovering and using new skills, acquiring knowledge about various things, and typically stepping outside of the comfort zone that you are used to. As you can imagine, this personal growth contributes to your overall development as an individual. You will literally grow as a person as a result, of meeting your goals.

They will also give you a better view of your life, the world, and what matters in the grand scheme of things. Goals almost always help you prioritize what truly matters in life. They guide your actions and decisions, helping you stay aligned with your values and aspirations.

Pursuing goals requires effective time management and prioritization. Successfully meeting goals can lead to better time management habits that can benefit various aspects of your life.

Achieving your goals provides opportunities for celebration and enjoyment. Taking the time to acknowledge your achievements and reward yourself can enhance your overall sense of well-being. In essence, meeting goals can lead to a sense of fulfillment, personal growth, and a positive impact on various areas of your life. It's a process that can contribute to your overall success and well-being.

Conclusion

Goals are one of the most important things to have in your life and, sadly, for people who have cluttered and busy brains, they can be very hard to achieve.

Without goals, you won't have progress. And without progress, you won't be able to make friends, create long-lasting relationships, and find a career. You need to have something to aspire to and goals can help you do that.

Many people don't understand how even the simplest goals can be hard when your brain is constantly being loud and disruptive and getting in your way. That is why you might have to take some extra steps to figure out, create, and follow through on your goals.

The good news is that now you know how to do that. And you also know how to work hard to clear your mind so that your biggest obstacle won't be in your way anymore. Can it be frustrating to be held back by your own brain? Of course it can be. It's unfortunate and not truly fair that you have to take extra steps to create and complete your goals. But it's not impossible. Plus, the more that you do it, the better you'll be.

Goals sometimes scare people because they feel so impossible to meet. But they shouldn't frighten you - they should excite you.

CHAPTER 5

Mindfulness

Throughout our book, we have talked about what it'll feel like when you have finally de-cluttered your mind and are able to live a life that isn't constantly barraged with unwanted thoughts, criticisms, and distractions. A life without so much noise coming from your brain is a very good one indeed.

One of the biggest problems that comes from a cluttered mind is that it doesn't allow you to focus on the here and now, the present time period. Instead, you're worried about what comes next, what path you're on, or how you appear in both past and future events. You lose any sense of mindfulness.

Mindfulness is essentially a mental state and practice that involves being fully present and engaged in the current moment, without judgment or distraction. It is a form of awareness that focuses on the present experience, including thoughts, emotions, sensations, and the surrounding environment. Mindfulness involves paying attention to the here and now with an open and accepting attitude, without getting caught up in past regrets or future worries. And you will notice that if you try to improve your sense of mindfulness, you will also be able to quiet your brain.

Mindfulness encourages you to observe your thoughts, feelings, and sensations as they arise in the present moment. This involves being fully engaged in whatever you're doing, whether it's a simple task or a complex activity.

Mindfulness involves accepting your thoughts, feelings, and experiences without labeling them as "good" or "bad." It's about observing these experiences with an open and non-judgmental attitude, allowing them to come and go without attachment.

Mindfulness helps you become more aware of your thought patterns, emotional reactions, and physical sensations. This increased awareness can lead to better understanding of yourself and your responses to different situations. It often involves focusing your attention on a specific object, breath, or sensation. We have spoken about mindfulness meditation before, when you keep your mind centered around an object or idea. Mindfulness is the practice of living your life in this same manner. It helps anchor your awareness to the present moment and prevents your mind from wandering.

Through mindfulness, you can develop the ability to respond to situations and challenges in a more thoughtful and deliberate manner, rather than reacting impulsively. It has been shown to reduce stress and anxiety and clear the brain by helping individuals detach from their worries and rumination. It encourages a more balanced and peaceful state of mind.

Regular mindfulness practice has been associated with improved overall well-being, increased emotional regulation, and greater life satisfaction. Practicing mindfulness can improve your ability to concentrate and stay focused on tasks, which can lead to increased productivity and better decision-making.

Mindfulness can be cultivated through various techniques and practices, some of which you can do in just a few minutes. It's important to note that mindfulness is a skill that can be developed over time with consistent practice. Many people find that incorporating mindfulness into their daily routines helps them manage stress, improve their mental clarity, and enhance their overall quality of life.

How To Achieve Mindfulness

Achieving mindfulness involves practicing specific techniques and approaches that help you cultivate present moment awareness and a non-judgmental attitude. It might not happen right away but it will happen, if you consistently work at it. Here are a few things to keep in mind when you are trying to quiet your brain and engage in staying in the current moment and observing the world around you.

Set Aside Time: First and foremost, you need to give yourself the proper amount of time to practice mindfulness. Much like working out or doing yoga, you should start by giving yourself an ample amount of time before you determine just how much you really need. Sometimes these exercises take a long time, sometimes it will go by quickly. To figure out how much time you need, look for a quiet and comfortable space where you won't be easily distracted. That is doubly important for you since you have a mind that can easily find distractions.

Choose a Technique: There are various mindfulness techniques you can try. Here are just a few of the ones that many people use:

Body Scan: Pay attention to different parts of your body, starting from your toes and moving up to your head. Notice any sensations or tension you may be experiencing. It helps sometimes if you picture yourself from out of your own body, looking down at yourself and observing every quadrant of your physical being.

Mindful Observation: Choose an object, such as a flower or a piece of fruit, and observe it closely. Notice its colors, shapes, textures, and any other details. Even the most minute details that don't seem important should be observed. Try to think of how you would describe the object, down to the tiniest details.

Mindful Walking: Take a slow and deliberate walk, paying attention to each step you take and the sensations in your feet and legs. Whether it be the smell of flowers, the sound of traffic or birds, the color of the trees and grass around you, make sure that you pay attention to everything you pass by. Again, imagine that you are going to describe it all to someone after you're done and it'll help you stay present and focused.

Focus on the Present: Whatever technique you choose, the goal is to bring your full attention to the present moment. Whenever your mind starts to wander, gently bring your focus back to the chosen point of attention. This is an important step for people who have cluttered minds because these types of brains can so easily jettison to the future or fall back into the past. But the past is gone and the future doesn't exist yet. You need to force your brain back to the here and now.

Non-Judgmental Awareness: As you practice mindfulness, allow your thoughts, feelings, and sensations to arise without judgment. Instead of labeling them as good or bad, simply observe them as they come and go.

Practice Regularly: Consistency is key to developing mindfulness. Set aside time for daily practice to gradually build your ability to stay present and attentive. You might not feel like you are making a lot of progress but you are.

Extend Mindfulness to Daily Activities: Beyond formal practice sessions, try to incorporate mindfulness into your everyday activities. Practice being fully engaged and present while eating, walking, or doing routine tasks. Even doing the dishes can help you stay mindful because you are doing a task. In many ways, it's like a form of meditation.

Be Patient and Kind to Yourself: Mindfulness is a skill that takes time to develop. Gently bring your focus back to the present whenever you notice your attention drifting.

Mindfulness Apps and Resources: There are many mindfulness apps and online resources that provide guided meditation sessions and tips for practicing mindfulness. These can be helpful, especially for beginners.

Mindfulness Classes or Workshops: Consider attending a mindfulness class or workshop to learn from experienced instructors and connect with a community of like-minded individuals.

Remember that mindfulness is a journey, and progress may be gradual. Over time, with consistent practice, you can develop greater awareness, emotional regulation, and a deeper sense of presence in your daily life. If you have found a method to achieve a quiet, less-cluttered mind, you need to keep it up and you need to work hard to continue a life without a busy brain. Practicing these mindfulness techniques are a great way to do just that.

Conclusion

Imagine your life without a cluttered brain.

Now, you may have days when it feels like things aren't going your way and your own brain is your biggest enemy. You feel nervous, you feel worried, you feel paranoid. You feel like you aren't performing well and that there is always something to worry about, even if you can't figure out what it is.

It'll feel like your brain is holding onto all sorts of information, especially things that don't matter anymore and, like a backpack full of excessive papers and school books, it is starting to weigh you down. You have a hard time staying present and maintaining relationships and keeping jobs can be very difficult. That is because your brain *is* working against you. It may have been this way for so long that you feel there is no way to overcome it. How can you stop your very own brain from getting in your way?

Well, it isn't always easy. And it almost always takes work and effort. But it is worth it.

So, again: imagine your life without a cluttered brain.

Instead of second-guessing yourself, you walk into every single situation with a strong belief in yourself. And even when you aren't around other people, your self-image is still strong.

Additionally, you are more capable when it comes to work, personal relationships, and more. No matter what situation you are in, you are present and focused on the here and now. The noise from your brain has been minimized and you find that what once challenged you so much doesn't anymore.

A cluttered brain can be a real pain and a true opponent of self-development, growth, peace and calm. But it doesn't have to be that way. Your days don't have to be filled with self-doubt and worry and a constant feeling of being distracted and filled with excessive thoughts. Instead, they can be composed of positive thinking, achieving your goals, and practicing techniques that sustain that good, peaceful feeling in your mind.

You have gone years and years with a brain that often gets in your way. It has become such a normal part of your existence that the thought of changing it at this point feels impossible. It's not. It's not impossible - there are many people who have been able to follow the steps and tips laid out in our book and have changed their perspective, calmed their brains, and lived a much more peaceful and happy life.

You can be a person who does that too. You know what you must do and, most importantly, you know that you can do it.